Bicycling Magazine's
600 Tips
for Better
Bicycling

By the Editors of *Bicycling* Magazine

Rodale Press, Emmaus, Pennsylvania

Compiled by *Ed Pavelka*

Edited by *Kathleen Becker*

Production editor: *Jane Sherman*

Copy editor: *Durrae Johanek*

Cover and interior design: *Lisa Farkas*

Cover photo: *John P. Kelly*

If you have any questions or comments concerning this book, please write:

Rodale Press
Book Reader Service
33 East Minor Street
Emmaus, PA 18098

Library of Congress Cataloging-in-Publication Data

Bicycling magazine's 600 tips for better bicycling / by the editors of Bicycling
     magazine
          p.   cm.
     ISBN 0-87857-936-2 paperback
     1. Cycling.   I. Bicycling!   II.   Title: Bicycling magazine's six hundred
tips for better bicycling.   III. Title: 600 tips for better bicycling.
IV. Title: Six hundred tips for better bicycling.
GV1041.B527   1991
796.6—dc20   90-25330
                                                                              CIP

Distributed in the book trade by St. Martin's Press

          8   10   9   7   paperback

CONTENTS

■ INTRODUCTION

You are holding what may be the most information-packed book ever written for the cyclist seeking improvement. Each chapter contains dozens of helpful tips—more than 600 in all—on every aspect of the sport. Whether you're looking for training advice, pointers on equipment and bike care, nutritional ideas for super performance, or guidance on racing or touring, you'll find these and much more presented in an accessible, enjoyable way.

Open to any page and begin browsing. You'll discover tips not only from *Bicycling's* staff of enthusiastic editor/riders but also from the biggest names in cycling. Among those whose knowledge we've tapped are Greg LeMond, Steve Bauer, Davis Phinney, John Tomac, Mark Gorski, Connie Carpenter Phinney, and other champions. Also contributing are the members of *Bicycling's* Fitness Advisory Board, which includes more than a dozen professionals from various branches of health and medicine. Still other expert advice was provided by two contributing writers and longtime students of the sport, Fred Matheny and Hank Barlow.

Of course, these tips are just that—nuggets of information to quickly increase your understanding of cycling and improve your performance. It's likely you'll also want in-depth advice, and for that we invite you to read any of the books in this cycling series or the magazine from which this book was derived. *Bicycling* and its special bonus section, *Mountain Bike*, have articles that go far beyond the basics to explore the training theories and technology shaping modern cycling.

Meanwhile, enjoy this collection of cycling wisdom. We guarantee that you'll learn something helpful on every page. Then go out and use it on your next ride.

Ed Pavelka, Executive Editor,
Bicycling Magazine

117 SKILL TONERS EVERY RIDER SHOULD KNOW

1. Joining a bike club is the best and quickest way for a new rider to learn firsthand about the sport.

2. When riding in a paceline, don't stare at the wheel in front. Look a couple of riders ahead and see what they're doing. Then you'll be prepared if something happens to make them veer or change speed. Remember, a paceline is like a Slinky. What happens at the front quickly trickles all the way to the back of the line.

3. For safety, don't brake in a paceline. Doing so will slow you too much, open a gap, and possibly cause a dangerous chain reaction. Instead, if you begin to overtake the rider in front, ease your pedal pressure, coast, sit up and catch more wind, or move out to the side a bit. Once you've lost enough speed, tuck back in line and smoothly resume pedaling.

4. Never overlap the rear wheel of another rider. If he or she should veer and strike your front wheel even lightly, you're likely to crash.

5. When taking the lead position in a paceline, don't accelerate. Maintain the same cadence as when drafting so you don't cause gaps to open between the other riders.

6. When leading a paceline up a hill, keep your cadence and pedal pressure constant by shifting to a lower gear. Standing and jamming is dangerous to the riders behind.

7. When you must stand on a climb, it's easy to decelerate and strike the front wheel of a following rider. If you favor your right leg, stand up just as it's beginning the down-stroke. Don't stand when you can't apply pressure at the same time. Since even good cyclists tend to do this in-correctly, try to notice who they are. Then when you're behind one and come to a hill, automatically drop back half a length.

8. When you start to tire, change your body position. Stand for a minute. Or sit if you're climbing out of the saddle. Alter your hand location on the bar.

9. Occasionally take one hand off the bar and shake it vig-orously to get the blood flowing and prevent numbness.

10. Always ride with your elbows bent and your arms and shoulders relaxed. This reduces fatigue caused by muscle tension and allows the arms to absorb some road shock, sparing your body.

11. Stretching on the bike also helps minimize fatigue. Coast, put your left foot down, then lean far to the right to stretch the back and left leg. Then do the right leg.

12. Know your fitness. "If you're in a race and there's an early break, you've got to decide whether to let them go and save a lot of energy for later, or go get them," says veteran pro racer Hugh Walton. "For this, you have to know how fit you are." In terms of recreational cycling, a realistic assessment of fitness might mean the difference between riding the full century or taking the 50-mile cutoff.

13. Pace yourself. Most races are won or lost in the last quarter because that's where fatigue takes its toll. The same is true for long training rides and events such as centuries. If you intend to go hard, wait until the last 25 percent of the ride. Then if you overestimate your strength and blow up, you won't have too many miles left.

14. Don't daydream. Always be aware of what's happening around you, whether in a race, on a group ride, or in traffic.

15. Former track stars Ian Jackson and Bruce Donaghy both

say riding in a velodrome increases your confidence in close quarters. "Your reflexes have to be a lot quicker on the track," Jackson explains. "You have to think ahead, to look ahead to the front of the bunch. You don't have brakes, and you can't stop pedaling."

16. Fast cornering on a wet road is a skill that not even every pro masters. Bruce Donaghy freely admits, "I despise racing in the rain. I just have an affinity for falling. But there are guys out there that, I swear, have a wheel on each side to keep them up. Hugh Walton, especially, is notorious for his ability in the rain." Walton explains: "I was a downhill ski racer, and I think it helped my bike racing. When you go through gates on skis, it's like riding through a corner in the rain. It's real important to line up for the corner correctly, and not pedal at the crucial time. Steer early, go through the corner straight, and steer again. In effect, make two little corners instead of one big one."

17. For wet roads, slightly deflate your tires to increase the size of their contact patch. For example, instead of using the full recommended pressure of about 110 psi, deflate them to about 90. Bleed just enough air so the tires deform slightly under your weight, but not so much that they squash like radial car tires.

18. You might try *increasing* tire pressure in the rain, especially for races. Why? Because then you'll have an advantage of 20 to 30 psi over those who let air out of their tires. Your rolling resistance will be down to the minimum while your competitors are squishing along the course on soft rubber. Our advice? Try it both ways, and always be careful.

19. Be especially cautious when rain begins, particularly if it's been dry for a few days. Oil and dust will float to the road surface, and make the road slick and treacherous. But as rain continues and washes this slippery stuff away, your tire's traction may become almost as secure as on a dry road. Nevertheless, painted lines and steel surfaces (manhole covers, grates, railroad tracks, bridge decks) are always slick when wet.

20. To get safely through a gravel-strewn corner, straighten up the bike until you're past the loose stuff, then resume turning. Avoid leaning the bike on a gravelly or sandy surface.

21. If you approach a turn too fast, don't lock the brakes. Instead, start coasting and raise the inside pedal so it won't strike the road when you lean the bike. Put your weight on the outside pedal. If you need to brake, do it with the rear wheel only before starting to turn.

22. To improve your chances of making it safely through a fast turn, keep your center of gravity low by staying down on the bike and pointing your inside knee into the turn. The key is being steady and smooth. If your wheels aren't jerking around, they'll hold traction better.

23. Don't be ashamed to reduce speed for turns, especially on wet roads. In most instances, European pros almost crawl through corners in the rain.

24. The ability to sprint, whether to escape a dog, cross an intersection ahead of traffic, or win a race, comes with practice. But such training can be painful drudgery unless you make a game of it. So hone your technique by sprinting for town limit signs during group training or recreational rides. It's an informal, fun way to put a little anaerobic training into a pleasure ride, without it being too competitive or regimented.

25. Don't downshift too soon on a hill. It will steal your momentum and you'll have to work harder.

26. Don't downshift too late on a hill. Instead of wasting energy by pushing a large gear and downshifting only after your legs are spent, keep your cadence within a comfortable range. If this is between 60 and 90 rpm, continue pedaling until your cadence starts to get slightly uncomfortable, say around 70 rpm. Then shift to a lower gear before you start to bog down.

27. Learn to do a trackstand and you may never again have to put a foot down at a stoplight. It's easiest when the pavement is sloping. When the slope is from right to left, place your right crankarm at 2 o'clock as you stop and turn the front wheel into the grade. (See illustration 1-1.)

Have your hands atop the brake lever hoods. The front wheel will try to roll backward down the slope, but by applying light pressure to the right pedal you'll counter this force and put the bike into a stalemate position. Voila! A trackstand. Reverse these instructions for a slope from the left. If the road is absolutely flat, you'll have to depend more on your balance and brakes.

Illustration 1-1. A trackstand.

28. For long hills, use a gear you can turn at about 80 rpm. This will be a relatively low gear that helps conserve energy for the entire climb, or you can upshift one cog as you near the top. As your strength increases, you'll be able to turn bigger gears at this cadence.

29. Whether you should sit or stand on climbs is a matter of personal preference. But generally, stay in the saddle on long, steady hills to conserve energy. On short ones, stand and jam to maintain speed.

30. Even though it's best to sit on a long climb, it's wise to

stand occasionally for a few dozen pedal strokes. This increases comfort by changing body position and altering which muscles are bearing the strain.

31. Cross railroad tracks near the side of the road. It's less worn there than in the center. Always cross with your wheels perpendicular to the rails, and be extremely careful if they're wet.

32. To smooth a jerky pedal stroke, practice pedaling down a long, gradual hill in a low gear (e.g., 42×17) as fast as possible without bouncing in the saddle.

33. Take a cue from fighters who shadowbox to refine technique. Early or late in the day, watch your shadow as you ride, checking for flaws in position, form, and pedaling style.

34. When climbing, think of yourself as pedaling across the stroke, rather than up and down. Strive to apply power from the back to the front. This maintains momentum while recruiting all your leg muscles.

35. To stave off fatigue during hard, sustained pedaling, learn to "float" each leg every three or four strokes. Let your foot fall without pushing. Legendary French time trial specialist Jacques Anquetil reportedly used this technique.

36. Develop bike-handling skills by riding with others on a grassy field. Play tag, ride the length of the field leaning into another rider, or pick up sticks without dismounting. Falling on soft ground won't hurt at slow speed.

37. Don't grasp the handlebar drops when climbing, because it compresses the diaphragm and inhibits breathing. Instead, use the bar top.

38. Always put your left foot down when stopping, to prevent chainring "tattoos" on your right leg.

39. If climbing isn't your forte, start hills at the front of the group and gradually drift back. This way, you'll still be with everyone at the top.

40. On a narrow road with no shoulder, take the lane to prevent cars from passing when it's not safe, then move over when opposing traffic clears.

41. Communication is the key to safe group rides. Make sure everyone knows of approaching turns, stops, and hazards by calling them out.

42. If you don't have a chance to slow for an obstacle such as railroad tracks or a pothole, pull on the handlebar to lift your front wheel over it. You may still damage your rear wheel, but at least you won't crash.

43. Shift with the upcoming terrain in mind. Stay on the large chainring if a descent is approaching, or shift to the small ring before a hill. Always be in the appropriate gear prior to a steep ascent.

44. To leave other riders behind, start a climb in a slightly lower gear than you need and shift up as you ascend.

45. Practice making a H-s-s-s-s-s, H-s-s-s-s-s sound to imitate a punctured tire. If done convincingly, you can get your rival to let up and look at his tires, giving you a chance to get away. (But you'd never do that, would you?)

46. When you're braking in the rain or anytime your rims are wet, remember that the first few wheel revolutions will only dry the rim and pads, so allow yourself more stopping distance. Once squeegeed dry, the brakes may suddenly take hold. Be ready to loosen your grip on the levers as soon as you feel the grab, or you could skid.

47. Normally, applying the front brake harder than the rear is the most efficient stopping technique. On slick roads, however, braking hard up front invites a front-wheel skid, which will almost certainly cause a crash. Better to risk a rear-wheel skid, since it's much easier to maintain control if that's the one that momentarily locks.

48. During an event, remember that a full water bottle weighs about a pound and a half. If you're approaching a long climb with two or three full bottles on your bike or person, drink your fill and dump all but the water you'll really need before the next stop or feed zone.

49. When descending, your bike will be more stable if you are pedaling, not just coasting. Always descend in high gear to retain the ability to accelerate if the situation calls for it.

50. Lower your saddle in winter. If you don't, your position will be too high because of the extra clothing you are sitting on.

51. Change your hand position often. Go from the tops of the lever hoods, to the hooks, to the drops . . . and all points between. Each change alters the angle of your back, neck, and arms, bringing some muscles more into play as others are stressed less. This is a key to comfort on long rides.

52. For a comfortable position that rests the arms by eliminating the need to grip with the hands, ride with the brake lever hoods between your index and middle fingers.

53. Ride with people who are a little stronger, faster, and more experienced. You'll learn a lot, and soon you'll be stronger and faster, too. Improvement is slow when you always ride alone or with people not as skilled.

54. Keep your tires clean. Even with Kevlar belts, it pays to brush the tread every few minutes. Use the leather palm of your gloves. Be careful doing the rear tire until you're oriented; a hand jammed between the spinning wheel and seat tube can cause a nasty spill.

55. Don't ride the brakes on a long descent. It will heat the rims and could cause a clincher tire to blow off, or a tubular's glue to melt. Instead, apply the brakes briefly and firmly to slow your speed, then coast until you want to slow again. This way the rims and brake pads will cool between applications.

56. Reduce your need to brake on descents by sitting up to let your body catch the wind. This can take 10 mph off your speed.

57. To stop high-speed shimmy, accelerate or decelerate from the point where it occurs. It also helps to lean forward, putting more weight on the front wheel, and to clamp the top tube between your knees.

58. When you enter a turn too fast, it's better to stand hard on your outside pedal and lean, lean, lean, rather than jam on the brakes, which will send you off-line. If your wheels slip and you go down, road rash is a much better fate than sailing across the lane into traffic or a tree.

59. When sprinting, take these tips from Canada's top pro rider, Steve Bauer.

- Don't move your upper body too much. Let your back serve as a fulcrum with your bike swaying back and forth beneath it.
- Don't center your weight too far forward. Your shoulders should not go past the front axle. Too much weight on the front wheel makes the bike unstable and hard to handle.
- Pull on the bar with a rowing motion to counter the power of your legs. This helps transfer your energy to the pedals rather than into wasted movement.

60. During a crash, the ideal response is to tuck your chin to your chest, cover your head with your arms, and roll. This will dissipate the force of the impact and protect your head—your most vulnerable body part, even if you're wearing a helmet. To make this response second nature, practice it by tumbling on a gym mat or soft grass.

61. If you ride at night, it's best to use two lights. One should be mounted low on the bike (fork or brake bolt) to cast a long beam along the road. The other should be on the handlebar or stem at motorists' eye level and point directly ahead to catch their attention. They'll barely notice a light pointed at the road.

62. If you normally ride at a fast pace, temper your speed at night to stay within the reaction zone of your headlight beam.

63. When cycling on a Friday or Saturday night, avoid main thoroughfares, particularly in the vicinity of bars and nightclubs. Drunk drivers are more plentiful at night, especially on weekends. Be extra cautious at intersections.

64. Don't fight to keep your speed in a headwind. Instead, use it as an opportunity to slow down and work on your pe-

daling form or, if you're with a group, to trade pulls efficiently with the others. In terms of pedaling effort, a cyclist
who travels 18 mph through calm air will have to work
about twice as hard to maintain this pace into a 10-mph
headwind.

65. Since your body accounts for approximately 70 percent of
wind resistance, your immediate response when turning
into the wind should be to become more aerodynamic by
hunkering down on the handlebar drops. Conversely, take
advantage of a tailwind by sitting upright and using your
body as a sail.

66. Because wind usually increases during the day, plan a
morning ride so your route takes you into a gentle breeze
that becomes a brisk tailwind on your return.

67. Beware of a crosswind from the left, because you naturally
lean into it in order to keep a straight line. Then when
traffic passes and momentarily blocks the wind, you may
steer into its lane. Help prevent this by keeping your elbows
and grip relaxed to enable quick responses to changing
forces.

68. If you have difficulty riding along the roadside in an un-
wavering line, try these pointers.

- Focus your eyes 20 feet ahead when riding at 10 to 15
  mph, and 1 foot farther for every additional mph. This
  will provide enough time to make smooth corrections
  when you see things in your way.
- Keep your hands, wrists, and elbows relaxed.
- Practice riding in a straight line on an empty parking
  lot or deserted country road by riding with your wheels
  on the painted lines. After you can ride without wavering, try it when you turn your head to look to the
  side and behind.
- When on busy roads, strive to ride an imaginary rail 6
  inches to the left of the white road-edge line.

69. The key to making it safely through unexpected patches
of sand or gravel is to stay relaxed. Resist the temptation
to jam on the brakes, and give the bike enough freedom
to drift in the direction it wants.

70. When coming upon a loose or bumpy surface, shift one gear higher and reduce your cadence. By pedaling slowly and steadily, you create a stable platform for your feet, which gives you more control than if you were coasting.

71. If forced from the road onto a soft shoulder, react instantly by sliding back on the saddle, reducing your cadence, and maintaining a firm yet sensitive grip on the handlebar. Continue on the shoulder until you find a safe and convenient "on ramp" back to the pavement.

72. The correct way to ride no-hands is to shift into a moderate gear and smoothly release the handlebar as you straighten your back and sit upright. Staying hunched forward puts too much weight over the front wheel and causes an erratic path down the road.

73. Perhaps the simplest way to stop an attacking dog when you can't outsprint it is to yell "No!" or "Go home!" Repeated several times in a strong voice, these commands mimic the dog's owner and may put an abrupt end to the chase.

74. Other ways to deal with a chasing dog are to squirt water from your bottle in its face, raise your tire pump menacingly (and swing it if you have to), or use a commercial dog repellent. The idea is to buy time until you can ride out of its territory.

75. If nothing works to stop a dog, get off your bike. Since it's the motion of the bicycle that seems to excite canines, this may end the threat. Keep your bike between you and the dog until it either wanders off or help arrives.

76. To optimize efficiency, think about pedaling in circles as you ride. Keep your knees in the same plane as the balls of your feet and consciously pull up with the pedals (if using toe straps or a step-in system).

77. For easier breathing that contributes to maintaining a low riding position and flat back, try this: Instead of actively drawing air into the lungs and then passively letting it out as in normal breathing, do the opposite—actively push air out and then passively let it in.

78.   As your effort becomes harder, increase the force of your breaths rather than their frequency.

79.   To make a panic stop, apply both brakes simultaneously, though you should emphasize the front one because it's more powerful. Using only the front brake may send you over the handlebar, and using only the rear will cause a skid and won't stop you fast enough. To counter the bike's tendency to pivot forward over the front wheel, slide off the back of the saddle with arms extended. (See photograph 1-1.)

Photograph 1-1. A panic stop.

80.   To help cultivate the fast, smooth spin it takes for a good sprint, do at least one ride per week in a 42 × 17 or lower gear.

81.   Here are 1984 Olympic champion Mark Gorski's six ways to enhance your ability to sprint at a moment's notice.
- Keep your toe straps fairly tight.
- Firmly grip the handlebar drops midway between the bend and the end.

- Keep your elbows slightly bent even when you're off the saddle, helping you ride a straight line.
- Pull evenly on the handlebar.
- Don't hold your breath, a common mistake during hard efforts.
- Keep your head up.

82. You'll sprint faster if you accelerate out of the saddle for 50 to 100 yards to reach maximum rpm, then sit and maintain your leg speed. This method will enable you to extend the sprint by as much as 200 yards.

83. When you make the transition from standing to sitting, gain valuable inches by pushing the bike forward as you drop to the saddle.

84. The trick to jumping the bike over something dangerous, such as a large crack in the road, is to begin with a deep crouch. Then sharply spring upward while lifting on the handlebar and pedals to pull the bike to your body. (Toe clips and straps or step-in pedals are mandatory.) Keep the front wheel straight so it will stay under you when landing.

85. To jump a wide object, such as a set of railroad tracks or cattle crossing, keep your speed up. If you hesitate or otherwise slow down and then decide to jump, the front wheel will make it across but the rear won't. In this case it's better to brake to walking speed, get off the saddle, and glide gingerly across the danger.

86. When descending through curves, follow an outside/inside/outside line. (See photograph 1-2.) This rule is based on simple geometry and is used not only in cycling but motor sports. It reduces the sharpness of the curve and minimizes the lean angle of the bike, making it the safest and quickest way through a downhill curve. For example, to negotiate a left-hand corner, approach the turn near the edge of the road, gradually move toward the centerline as its apex approaches (traffic permitting), and then ease back toward the edge of the road as the corner eases. Conversely, a right-hand turn requires a centerline/berm/centerline course.

Photograph 1-2. A descending curve.

87. In weather so cold that even insulated footwear doesn't prevent your toes from becoming numb, use an old cyclocross trick: Get off your bike and walk or run for a minute every half hour.

88. To become confident when riding in a paceline, start by staying one bike length from the rider in front of you, then gradually close the gap as your experience and ability increase. Once you can ride comfortably within a wheel's length, you'll be enjoying the effects of drafting.

89. The next time another rider passes you, move over into his or her draft. Without any extra effort, your speed will increase, if only temporarily.

90. You may be right when you feel that no matter which way you turn, the wind is always against you. Only those winds within the trailing 160 degrees of an imaginary circle drawn around a cyclist provide assistance, whereas wind anywhere in the other 200 degrees works to slow you.

91. To develop a fast spin, descend in a lower-than-usual gear. This will force your legs to spin fast and train your motor system to perform at speed.

92. When riding in the drops, grip the curved rather than the flat part of the bar. Holding it near the ends rotates your wrists downward and inhibits control.

93. When riding one-handed for any reason, your hand should be on top of the bar, next to the stem. If your hand is farther out from the stem, the bike is more likely to veer unexpectedly if the front wheel hits a rock, bump, or pothole.

94. Ride rough pavement with your hands atop the bar. Lean forward and use your arms to support upper-body weight. Keep your elbows bent outward, use your arms as shock absorbers, and allow the bike to shake and rattle freely beneath you. Make sure your thumbs are under the bar rather than over it, so a sharp bump won't bounce your hands off.

95. Take this climbing tip from Davis Phinney, the pro sprinting specialist who made himself into a strong enough ascender to win the mountainous Coors Classic: The first step is developing correct form and breathing habits. This will help any rider improve significantly in a short time.

96. Follow these rules to improve your basic climbing technique.

- Relax your shoulders. Keep them down and back so your chest is open for full, deep breathing. Relaxed shoulders also keep the upper body supple, enabling it to move smoothly with the pedaling motion.
- Keep your back flat and your elbows bent. This is true whether you're climbing from the seated or standing position. Like hunched shoulders, a curved back restricts the diaphragm and limits your intake of oxygen.
- Grip the handlebar lightly. Most often, your hands should rest on the top of the bar near the stem. When more steering control is needed, or before standing, move your hands to the brake lever hoods. Don't use the handlebar drops for climbing unless you're sprinting uphill.
- Stay seated whenever possible. Climbing out of the saddle usually induces a higher heart rate and, therefore, requires more energy (at the same speed) than staying seated. Stand only when you can't generate enough power in the saddle. Or, on long climbs, stand periodically to stretch your muscles and enhance cir-

culation, even if the steepness of the grade doesn't require it.

- When you must stand, move like a cat. Rise smoothly from the saddle without disturbing the bike's forward motion. Doing it right will conserve energy and preserve your rhythm.

97. During a climb, choose your gears wisely. If you're out of the saddle and bobbing excessively as you pedal, your gear is too low, causing you to drive the pedals through their power stroke too quickly. Conversely, if you must throw the bike excessively from side to side to accommodate the force needed to turn the pedals, your gear is too high.

98. Use a weight training program to build your climbing power. Squats or leg presses should be the centerpiece of your program. These exercises build power in the quadriceps, calves, and buttock muscles. For the upper body, rowing exercises develop the strength to pull on the handlebar and balance the force being exerted by the legs.

99. Here are eight commonsense tips for keeping friendly drivers friendly.

- Keep right. If there's a wide, clean, safe shoulder, use it. One thing that always irritates motorists is a cyclist riding in the middle of the road for no apparent reason.
- If riding with a partner, ride side by side only when it won't cause traffic to back up or pass dangerously.
- Don't force vehicles to repass you needlessly. At a stop light, stay behind the last car instead of going ahead of drivers who may have just had difficulty passing you safely. Next time, they might not be so careful.
- Ride predictably. Keep a straight line when you're cruising, and use hand signals when turning or changing lanes.
- Stay off busy roads. Drivers will be uptight enough without you being in their way. Find an alternate route out of the main traffic flow.
- Make yourself visible. It's a courtesy and plain good sense to wear brightly colored clothes.
- Avoid "provocative" actions. Don't circle in front of a car or lean on it while waiting for a light.

- Be gracious. Motion a driver to make his turn in front of you if you'll be slow getting under way. Who knows? That driver might look a bit more favorably on the next cyclist down the road.

100. During long descents on wet roads, maintain slight brake pad contact with the rims to keep them free of excess water and allow quicker stopping.

101. Never ride through a puddle if you can avoid it. It's not uncommon to find a gaping hole under the water.

102. To perform a cyclocross, or off-road, dismount, shift to the gear you'll need beyond the hurdle. Swing your right leg backward over the bike, and bring it between your left leg and the frame. Continue moving your right foot forward. Before it hits the ground, kick your left foot out of the toe clip. All of a sudden, you're running.

103. To remount as you're running beside the bike, place both hands on the bar and jump onto the saddle in one fluid motion. Hit the seat with the inside of your thigh, then slide to your normal position. Try to put your feet into the toe clips without looking at them.

104. Proper pedaling technique will improve your performance and help keep you injury-free, so it's important to spend some time making sure you're doing it right. The first step is to be certain your position on the bike is correct. Then, according to recent biomechanical research, the ideal pedaling technique involves the application of force in a perpendicular direction to the crankarm. You should pedal in smooth circles, exerting the greatest force on the downstroke. Then, to minimize the dead point at the bottom, pull back on the pedal during the upstroke.

105. When time trialing, use your arms to help stabilize your hips and buttocks on the saddle. Try to push slightly on the bar without using your upper back or shoulder muscles. Don't pull—it uses energy and is only necessary during sprints and climbs.

106. Always keep your elbows close to your body. When they're bowed you become less aerodynamic and you could bump another rider.

107. Drafting just one rider when going 25 mph gives you the same advantage as drafting two or more. Illustration 1-2 shows data gathered at the University of Florida, where 28 racing cyclists took part in a study designed to quantify the precise benefits of drafting. The percentages are the reduction in VO_2 max—the measurement of aerobic capacity—of the gray riders compared to riding alone at the same speed.

Drafting one rider at 20 mph 18%   Drafting 2 or 4 riders at 25 mph:
At 23 or 25 mph: 27%   27%

Pack riding at 25 mph: 39%   Drafting a pickup at 25 mph: 62%

Illustration 1-2. The benefits of drafting.

108. On long and/or gradual climbs, remain seated and shift your weight toward the back of the saddle. This extends your legs slightly, which fosters power and may allow use of a larger gear for more speed.

109. When sprinting or accelerating a big gear, use your arms in a coordinated manner with the rest of your body. Pull against the left part of the bar when the left foot is pushing down on the pedal. At the same time, apply enough counterforce with your right arm to keep from turning the front wheel. As the right leg begins its downward stroke, reverse this process.

110. Be ready for quicker handling and oversteer when using an aerodynamic handlebar or clip-on attachment. This happens because riding in such an extended position puts more weight on the front wheel.

111. Whenever possible, breathe through your nose. It warms, filters, and humidifies air better than the mouth. But when riding hard you need more oxygen and must breathe through your mouth. This is the natural way and works best for most riders, despite the proponents of various forced-breathing patterns.

112. Even the best lock won't save your bike unless it's used properly. Make your bike less of a target by locking it in a well-lit area. Always secure the frame and the wheels, and examine the object you're locking them to. Ideally, it should be a metal post, such as a parking meter, with something affixed to the top to prevent your bike from being lifted off. Thieves won't hesitate to steal your bike and lock and separate them later.

113. U-locks are popular and effective, but they require a special technique. First, remove the front wheel and rest the frame's fork tips on the ground. Next, place the front wheel parallel to the rear one. The U encloses the two rims, seat tube, and post (or whatever you're locking it to). Finally, the crossbar is attached.

114. Whatever type of lock you use, don't place it near the ground. In this position it's easier for a thief to apply leverage with tools or crush it with a hammer.

115. When your chain derails in front, don't immediately dismount. Instead, try gently shifting it back on while pedaling. If this doesn't work, you needn't dirty your hands. Invert the bike so the chain catches on the bottom of the small chainring. Then grasp the pedal and turn it backward to fully engage the chain.

116. Use the whole saddle during rides. Sit in the center for normal pedaling, scoot forward to increase your spin, and slide back to power up a hill.

117. The way you ride can determine how well your road bike's wheels hold up. Sharp impacts can cause flats and damage rims, so always stand and bend your knees and elbows like a jockey to absorb the shock when riding over railroad tracks, potholes, etc.

94 TRAINING BOOSTERS

1. Racers should train by time, not miles, says Greg LeMond. The reason? "Twenty miles into a headwind is a lot different than 20 with a tailwind."

2. "Use your intelligence" in determining how far and long to train, says Greg LeMond. Cyclists who work full time or go to school should probably limit their training to 10 or 12 hours a week "because you need some time in your life for other things. I think your mind will burn out before your body. Your body can adapt to almost anything."

3. Ride rollers in the winter to develop a fluid pedaling style. Although some people say you're intrinsically smooth or you're not, you can train for it by concentrating on making a circular stroke while pedaling at a high cadence.

4. Resistance trainers are beneficial in winter, too. Whatever you use, pedal daily for 20 or 30 minutes at an intensity that raises your heart rate to 70 or 80 percent of its maximum. Winter gives you a psychological rest by reducing your riding time, but you mustn't let your cardiovascular system get out of shape.

5. Greg LeMond recommends using a heart rate monitor to gauge your effort. He trains at 65 to 80 percent of his maximum heart rate for endurance; at 80 to 90 percent for sustained, intense efforts; and at 90 to 100 percent for sprints and short intervals. "Below 65 percent, you might as well stay home," he says.

6. When training by heart rate, ignore workouts based on gears, LeMond says. The fitter you are, the higher the gear that's necessary to achieve your target heart rate.

7. Maintain a smooth, fast cadence while training on the road. Racers spin to get more flexibility and suppleness in their muscles. They train in easier gears, so when it's time to go hard they can use a bigger gear without it hurting as much. European pros will roll along in 53×18 or 53×17 for 5 or 6 hours at a time.

8. LeMond couples power with smoothness by concentrating on pulling back on each pedal as it comes through the bottom of the stroke. He says to imagine you're scraping mud off your shoe.

9. Take your time warming up on the bike. For example, it may take 30 to 45 minutes to feel ready to go hard. Stretching before riding, however, may help reduce this time.

10. At the start of a long training ride, go into the wind. This way, you can ride faster coming back even if you're tired, and you won't be chilled by a stiff breeze.

11. The best way to recover from a hard effort is to ride easily the next day rather than take the day off. Use the opportunity to cycle with family and friends who are normally "too slow."

12. For a fun and unique diversion from cycling, try "skiing" on pavement with in-line skates such as Rollerblades. They're compact, easy on your knees and, most important, strengthen the cycling muscles.

13. When doing quality training such as intervals, use a heart rate monitor. Determine your anaerobic threshold by observing at what heart rate you can time trial for 5 miles. Then do intervals in a range 10 percent below this rate.

14. Carry $5 and some change in your tire repair kit. You can buy a snack on long rides, phone home if you have a breakdown, or pay a driver to drop you off.

15. If you hate headwinds, plan routes that avoid them. Use mountains, tree lines, valleys, and houses to shield you until you turn around and can enjoy a tailwind.

16. For late-afternoon training that may extend to dusk, carry two reflective leg bands, a portable light, and a reflective triangle or vest in your jersey pocket so you can get home safely.

17. If you train late in the day when the temperature dips, carry a 2×2-foot piece of plastic folded in a pocket. When you begin to chill, stuff the sheet up the front of your jersey to insulate your chest. This also works for long descents in mountainous regions.

18. On long rides for endurance, throw in a couple of 15-second sprints every 45 minutes or so. You'll relieve saddle pressure, add variety, and develop speed.

19. Don't be afraid to occasionally push a real big gear. Wait until you're warmed up and conditions are right—tailwind or long downgrade—then go for it. Besides feeling the thrill of power and speed, you'll be developing the strength it takes to still make good time should the wind turn or the road slant upward.

20. During the season, take 10 minutes twice a week after riding to do upper-body strength maintenance exercises such as pull-ups, push-ups, crunchers for the abdominals, and neck isometrics.

21. Fit training into weekend family outings by cycling one way as everyone else travels by car.

22. To help pass time on an indoor trainer, play games with a heart rate monitor. Try to reach 140 (then recover), 150 (recover), then 160. For a medium-intensity workout, simply go back and forth from 130 to 150.

23. When finishing a lower-body winter weight training program, go directly to intervals and climbing workouts on the bike. Hold off on endurance training until later in the spring. If you immediately follow your leg strengthening progress with a month or more of slow-paced endurance rides, you'll lose some of the power you gained.

24. If a riding companion is too slow, use a tandem. You can pedal as hard as you like, but you'll never drop your stoker.

25. If you have less than an hour to train, emphasize quality. Warm up by spinning easily for 10 minutes. Do five 15-second sprints with 45 seconds between them, then 10 intervals comprising one minute on and one minute off. Cool down for 10 minutes.

26. If you're bored with a training route, ride it in the opposite direction. You'll be amazed how different it seems.

27. In bad spring weather, ride a mountain bike on the road. You'll save your road bike from rust and build power pushing the heavier bike and fat tires.

28. To put more fun and variety in winter training, try cyclocross. This is off-road riding using either a modified road bike (low gears and $700 \times 35C$ knobby tires) or mountain bike. It's typically done on a hilly obstacle course that requires some dismounting and running with the bike. It's a great cardiovascular workout that develops bike-handling skills, and the lifting and carrying strengthens the upper body.

29. Successful riders approach cycling as a year-round activity. But this doesn't mean to simply go out and ride every day. Instead, use a comprehensive month-by-month approach to provide variety and all the elements necessary for maximizing your potential in competition or even lower-key fast recreational events such as centuries. Here is a calendar of programs to follow.

- **January/February: body preparation.** Now is the time to build overall strength, because the foundation for your season is established in the dead of winter. Alternate easy cycling indoors on a resistance trainer or on the road with aerobics, weight training, running, cross-country skiing, and sports such as basketball. This will condition your whole body to handle the more intense cycling workouts to follow.
- **March: power and skill.** The emphasis shifts to cycling with the use of a cyclocross or mountain bike for the off-road work that will help you develop power and bike-handling skills. You'll want to continue aerobic-paced road rides, too, when weather permits. Otherwise, pedal away on the indoor trainer.
- **April: aerobic base.** Temperatures are warming, daylight is increasing, and the racing season is near. Continue to build your base of aerobic miles and begin venturing into the hills. The ascents are where you develop the muscle strength that's necessary not only for climbing, but for faster riding on the flat.

- **May: speed.** Time to build a faster top end for those midsummer criteriums, as well as the finishing sprint in races or competitive group rides. It comes in handy when the Doberman is out, too. Sprints, fartlek, interval training, and spirited group rides are all useful tools.
- **June: peaking.** At the height of the season you need to know how to peak for certain events, whether they're races or long and fast recreational rides. This means converting your solid base of cycling fitness into selected short periods of super performance.
- **July: remedial work.** By now you have ridden enough to know what you do well and where you need to improve. July is the time to identify your deficiencies in sprinting, climbing, time trialing, endurance, or tactics and work to improve them.
- **August: criterium skills.** Many clubs sponsor weekly criteriums during August, and the USCF race calendar is full of these short, fast events. To be successful, you need to improve your tactics, bike handling, speed, and sprint. Doing so will make you a more proficient rider all the time.
- **September/October: endurance.** As racing winds down, many of us like to ride centuries or go on long one-day outings with club mates or alone. This is the time of year to hone the techniques and stamina for these lengthy efforts. The endurance base that's built will even stay with you until the following season if you follow it up with a sound winter program.
- **November/December: active rest.** You've had a great season and are raring to go for the next one. But be careful—now is the time when the seeds of overtraining and chronic fatigue are sown. Relax from the rigors of the busy summer and fall by enjoying some active rest. Noncycling sports, weight training, and easy, no-pressure rides will rejuvenate your mind and body for next season.

30. Beginning with your next workout, start a training diary. It doesn't have to be expensive or elaborate; all you need is space to record pertinent data each day. This will allow you to objectively analyze and learn from your satisfying progress or frustrating failures.

31. To become an efficient user of fat for fuel, go on steady rides for at least 2 hours. Fat needs oxygen to burn, and endurance training puts the oxygen where you need it—in your muscles. The longer you go, the more you'll adapt your body to run on fat. Try for at least two such rides per week.

32. One of the best ways to get a total body workout in a short time during winter—and have fun, too—is with regular aerobic workout at a local health club. Pro racer Ron Kiefel is just one rider who has taken advantage of the varied demands of exercise classes.

33. Now a few words for anyone who needs more power for climbing and time trialing (and who doesn't?): squats and leg presses. Either exercise is a great builder of strength in the quadriceps (the large muscles in front of the thighs) and gluteus maximus (buttocks muscle). These are the primary muscles for pushing the pedals with greater power.

34. The key to building muscle strength for cycling is to perform numerous repetitions with light to moderate weights. This will also increase your muscle endurance without adding bulk.

35. If you live in a snowy climate, don't curse the white stuff that keeps you off the bike. Dive right in on cross-country skiing. It's a great builder of aerobic power and upper-body strength. It conditions most of the leg muscles required by cycling, and the equipment is relatively inexpensive. Two of its biggest advocates are Greg LeMond and Andy Hampsten.

36. If you live where you must resort to lots of indoor cycling during winter, consider investing in an ergometer. They're stable, quiet, and you won't be sweating all over your bike.

37. If you're serious about racing, ask your doctor where you can take a VO_2 max test. This will the best predictor of your potential in cycling and other endurance sports. VO_2 max, the measurement of your body's aerobic capacity, is the amount of oxygen you can take in and use during a 1-minute period. The figure is dependent on body type and the quantity of oxygen you are able to inhale. Heredity plays an important role, as do fitness and physical maturity. Elite road racers may consume 80 milliliters of oxygen per kilogram of body weight (the measurement for VO_2 max), while average in-shape riders may be in the 50s.

38. Commute by bike. This is the best way to include cycling—and a few more of those valuable miles—in your everyday activity.

39. Don't train hard more than twice a week. Whether you are doing formal interval training, speed play (fartlek), club races, or tackling big hills, this is stress on the body, and too much will wear you down. If you separate such efforts with at least two days of low-gear, high-rpm pedaling that assists recovery, the result should be exactly what you want—greater speed and strength.

40. Take a rest one day each week. A day off refreshes your body and mind. Use your normal riding time that day for bike maintenance.

41. Be aware of the warning signals of overtraining, a condition of chronic fatigue that can devastate any enthusiastic rider, not just racers. Among the tip-offs are an elevated resting heart rate, weight loss, poor sleep patterns, irritable disposition, an I-don't-care attitude, a lingering cold, aching legs, and general lifelessness.

42. Entering the new season, spin for about a thousand miles before you start pushing big gears or climbing steep hills. That's the rule subscribed by most racers, and it makes sense for everyone. High-cadence, low-gear riding is what sets the foundation for injury-free work in the big chainring.

43. To develop the ability to quickly accelerate to high speed, do "speedwork" once a week. This is a training session based on a thorough warm-up, then several all-out bursts to top speed interspersed with easy riding for full recovery.

44. To improve your maximal oxygen uptake (VO_2 max) and develop your ability to sustain fast riding, do "intervals" once a week. Following a warm-up, accelerate to a speed that's as hard as you can go for a specified time (usually 15 to 90 seconds). Then ride easier for 30 to 60 seconds to partially recover. Repeat several times, then ride easily to cool down.

45. Even if you just ride for fitness but would like to come closer to your potential, intervals can help. They'll improve your ability to match the pace on club rides while helping you surmount those little rolling hills that seem to be everywhere. If you're interested in racing, though, intervals are essential.

46. If you are a racer, do intervals twice a week, separating the workouts by at least 48 hours. If your important or longest rides occur on the weekends, the best days for interval training are Tuesdays and Thursdays.

47. The training method called "peaking" will help you ride at your best in a special event. It requires good all-around cycling fitness, then a four-week schedule of special preparation. The first two weeks should consist of hard training with racing or long rides on the weekends. The goal is to dig deep into your reserves of strength, which will cause you to rebound to a much higher performance peak if you rest adequately. So, train easily during the third week to recover. Start the final week with hard rides for the first three or four days, then switch to short, easy spinning. After the big event, go easy for a week to fully recuperate.

48. In general, three peaks in one season is the most anyone should try. A physical peak is just one step from a tumble into overtraining.

49. Never take the day off before a race. If you need rest, do it two days before. Take a short ride on the eve of the event, and include a couple of sprints to make sure your bike and body are operating well.

50. To improve endurance, do one long ride each week. The key is to maintain a steady, brisk pace for the distance. If you wear a pulse monitor, try to go the whole way at 75 to 80 percent of your maximum heart rate. Make sure your diet contains plenty of high-quality carbohydrates to fuel long efforts, and eat frequently during such rides.

51. To improve power, head for the hills. Once a week, do repeats up a half-mile hill, resting on the way down. Go fast enough to put yourself into oxygen debt during the 15 to 30 seconds before you reach the top. Use a gear you can turn at about 80 rpm.

52. To improve speed, accelerate as fast as you can for distances from 100 to 300 yards in a moderately high gear. Get off the saddle, charge down the road as you build cadence, then sit and keep increasing your rpm. Make several such efforts during one workout each week.

53. If you have limited time to train, make every second count. Prepare your bike the evening before, and lay out your riding clothes. Or ride during your lunch hour and snack later back at the desk. If you emphasize quality by keeping your heart rate high, you'll be amazed at how much improvement you can pack into an hour.

54. Off-season aerobic training, whether indoor cycling or another sport, is very important: Two weeks of inactivity will result in a noticeable loss of your strength and flexibility, in addition to a nominal weight gain. And in 8 to 12 weeks, the cardiovascular strides you made during the season will be all but erased.

55. Cross-country skiing is beneficial to cyclists because it builds powerful quadriceps and other leg muscles, as well as the upper body. And skiers traditionally are among the world's best-conditioned endurance athletes.

56. Swimming improves flexibility and upper-body strength. It's also great for building leg and hip strength without overly stressing tendons and muscles. To gain cardiovascular benefits, work out at your training heart rate for at least 20 minutes three times a week.

57. Running's benefits transfer to cycling if you run uphill or on stairs. This will strengthen your quads and calves, and it's a great cardiovascular conditioner. Two cautions: Walk (don't run) down hills to prevent knee injury, and begin a running program slowly to avoid undue soreness, then run no more frequently than every other day.

58. Indoor trainers are a good way to maintain a degree of cycling fitness in winter, but you'll do better to ride outdoors as much as possible. This way you'll also develop important

riding skills such as keeping a straight line, cornering, or descending, which you can't master inside.

59. If you're out of shape and just getting started in cycling, begin slowly. Initial rides, whether outside or on an indoor trainer, should be limited to 20 to 30 minutes three days a week. Pedal briskly, but don't get out of breath. As fitness increases, begin riding five days a week for at least 30 minutes, and progress from there.

60. Not everyone has the good fortune to train under a coach who designs daily workouts and yearly programs. If you don't, follow these seven steps to successful self-coaching.

A. Set goals. However lofty or modest your aims, you need to identify them and write them down. When your goals are firmly set, every training day has a purpose.

B. Evaluate your basic talent. Do this objectively and honestly. The world would be a dreary place without dreams, but make sure yours are rooted in reality.

C. Evaluate your strengths and weaknesses. A good training plan will maximize your cycling talents and remedy your shortcomings.

D. Ask questions. Get information from experienced cyclists. The most helpful are those who have studied the sport for several years and ride intelligently to maximize less-than-outstanding physical talent.

E. Record your workouts. Keep a training diary so you can duplicate workouts that precede a hot streak. Conversely, when you ride poorly you'll know what training pattern to avoid.

F. Chart your improvement. Getting better is the name of the game. To be sure your program is working, you need an accurate account of your progress toward greater endurance (century rides) and speed (club time trials).

G. Add spice to your training. Vary your schedule so you aren't doing the same thing every day, week, and month. And remember that several days away from the bike once in a while can revitalize your attitude and performance.

61. Don't overcoach yourself. In cycling, careful attention to detail will make you better—to a point. You want to be dedicated, not obsessive. Work on your weaknesses, but never forget that the best reason for riding a bike is to have fun.

62. Even if you're primarily a road rider, using a mountain bike is one of the best ways to build riding skills and fitness. A weekly off-road outing will help improve your balance, control, and confidence, plus develop your strength from powering up steep climbs.

63. To calculate cadence (pedal revolutions per minute), count the number of times your right foot reaches the bottom of the pedal stroke in 15 seconds, then multiply by four.

64. To find your most efficient pedaling cadence you'll need a cyclecomputer, a heart rate monitor, a calm cool day, and a mile-long stretch of flat road. After warming up, ride the course several times in different gears while keeping your speed the same. For example, do each run at 18 mph. Record the maximum heart rate attained and the cadence required to hold your target speed. The trial in which your heart rate is lowest will indicate your "ideal" cadence. Match the results with another test seveal days later, reversing the gear sequence to nullify the effect fatigue may have on your heart rate.

65. Experiment with different cadences for different terrains and wind conditions, looking for an rpm that maximizes speed while minimizing muscle fatigue and breathlessness. It may be 75 or 95, and it may change as you become fitter and your pedaling technique improves.

66. More reasons to train with a heart rate monitor: It helps you avoid riding too intensely on recovery days or too easily when you should be pushing your limits. It also helps you avoid ride after ride in the murky middle, where returns aren't great for the time spent.

67. Use a monitor to correlate heart rate with subjective feelings of fitness and recovery. After a warm-up of several miles, ride up a familiar hill and decide which of the following applies to you.

- Legs are tired and pulse is higher than normal.
- Legs are tired but pulse is normal or low.
- Legs are fresh but pulse is higher than normal.
- Legs are fresh and pulse is normal or low.

In the first case, keep the ride short and easy. The second and third cases indicate incomplete recovery from previous rides, making it wise to moderate the pace, distance, and terrain. The fourth case tells you that you're ready for hard training.

68. The key to training with a heart rate monitor is knowing what your heart's maximum is. To get a very rough estimate, subtract your age from 220. If possible, have your maximum heart rate determined with a stress test or VO_2 max test. Once you have this figure, training becomes a matter of percentages using these four levels of exertion.

- 60 to 65 percent of maximum heart rate to promote recovery
- 75 percent of maximum to build aerobic endurance
- 85 percent of maximum to approach your anaerobic threshold, the point at which the greatest aerobic improvement occurs
- 95 to 100 percent of maximum, done in short bursts to train for sprints, chases, hill jams, and so on

69. If you always keep your heart rate above the 60 to 65 percent level during your workout, you will always be improving your fitness.

70. Tree-trunk thighs do not guarantee an explosive sprint. You also need strong back, shoulder, and chest muscles. Without a balance of upper- and lower-body muscles, the legs tend to control the bike, making it difficult to accelerate smoothly.

71. Rollers seem old fashioned compared with modern resistance trainers, but they may still be the best way to develop a smooth, circular pedal stroke. You'll know you've got it when you can keep the front tire on one spot, as if there's a groove in the roller. As long as the wheel meanders, keep working on it.

72. You don't need to do 100-mile-long rides to train for a century. Table 2-1 shows two proven training schedules to use during the ten weeks leading up to the event. The first assumes you've been riding an average of 45 to 50 miles per week and will enable you to complete a century. If you've been averaging more than 75 miles per week, try the second schedule. It'll help you achieve a personal-best performance.

In each schedule, "easy" means a leisurely ride, mainly to recover from a previous day's hard workout; "pace" means simulating the speed you want to maintain for the century; "brisk" means a lively tempo that's faster than century pace. If your century is on a Saturday, move back the final week's training one day.

TABLE 2-1.
Schedule 1
Goal: To Ride 100 Miles

Week	Mon.	Tues.	Wed.	Thurs.	Fri.	Sat.	Sun.	Total Weekly Mileage
	Easy	Pace	Brisk		Pace	Pace	Pace	
1	6	10	12	Off	10	30	9	77
2	7	11	13	Off	11	34	10	86
3	8	13	15	Off	13	38	11	98
4	8	14	17	Off	14	42	13	108
5	9	15	19	Off	15	47	14	119
6	11	15	21	Off	15	53	16	131
7	12	15	24	Off	15	59	18	143
8	13	15	25	Off	15	65	20	153
9	15	15	25	Off	15	65	20	155
10	15	15	25	Off	10	5 Easy	100	170

(continued)

TABLE 2-1.—*Continued*
Schedule 2
Goal: A Century with Strength to Spare

Week	Mon.	Tues.	Wed.	Thurs.	Fri.	Sat.	Sun.	Total Weekly Mileage
	Easy	Pace	Brisk		Pace	Pace	Pace	
1	10	12	14	Off	12	40	15	103
2	10	13	15	Off	13	44	17	112
3	10	15	17	Off	15	48	18	123
4	11	16	19	Off	16	53	20	135
5	12	18	20	Off	18	59	22	149
6	13	19	23	Off	19	64	24	162
7	14	20	25	Off	20	71	27	177
8	16	20	27	Off	20	75	29	187
9	17	20	30	Off	20	75	32	194
10	19	20	30	Off	10	5 Easy	100	184

73. If you train by heart rate, take the weather into account. According to a university study, when it's 32°F, your heart beats about 10 percent slower. Thus, if you maintain your regular training heart rate when it's cold, you'll be getting a workout that's 10 percent more intense. Or, conversely, you can go 10 percent below your normal training heart rate and still derive the usual benefits.

74. Even a new rider who has no racing ambitions can benefit from a weekly program that includes both speed and distance. In order to firm your legs, lose weight, and be healthier, use a program that combines the following workouts.

- Moderate days. To lose weight, forget about the stopwatch and ride medium distances at a comfortable pace.

This will burn fat, as opposed to the carbohydrates that fuel short, intense efforts.
- Endurance day. To improve your stamina, go on one long ride every week. Don't worry about time, just complete the distance.
- Speed days. These are crucial to cardiovascular improvement and muscle tone. Twice a week, for example, try to complete 15 miles in an hour while maintaining a cadence of 85 to 90 rpm. Gradually increase speed and distance as you become fitter.

75. Despite its many benefits, cycling neglects to strengthen several of your muscles. Here is a list of muscles you should exercise and develop to improve your performance.
- Abdominals. They're crucial for stabilizing your riding position and balancing the lower-back muscles that are often highly developed in cyclists.
- Neck and trapezius. These muscles support your head on long rides and protect your spinal cord in a crash.
- Pectorals and triceps. Strength here will help prevent upper-body fatigue caused by leaning on the handlebar for long periods.
- Deltoids. These are large triangular muscles that cover the shoulder joint and protect it in a fall.
- Latissimus dorsi. In conjunction with the biceps, lats provide the necessary arm strength to pull on the handlebar in sprints or on extended climbs.

76. The biggest problem that many cyclists face is finding enough time for training amid life's many responsibilities. Here are ten ways to do it.
- Train before work.
- Ride at lunch.
- Commute by bike.
- Train at night.
- Schedule your ride like any other daily appointment.
- Train intensely to maximize limited time.
- Adjust your goals to reflect limited time.
- Enlist your family's support so you can ride without guilt.

- Combine your cycling with family activities.
- Ride indoors when bad weather or interruptions occur.

77. Avoid total layoffs. During the first couple of weeks, your fitness will deteriorate remarkably fast. A rule of thumb is that the biomechanical changes that occurred in the muscle with training decline in what is called a half-time of 12 days. This means that in only 12 days you'll go halfway from your trained state to the level you'd be if you had never trained at all. And you'll go another half of that distance between 12 and 24 days.

78. When you realize that your training schedule will be disturbed for more than a couple of weeks, embark on a minimum maintenance program to keep from regressing. The key is to train intensely at least two days a week. This will maintain your maximal oxygen uptake and your ability to perform all-out efforts of 6 to 8 minutes.

79. For losing weight, stationary cycling is just as effective as other indoor sports, according to university researchers. They compared it to rowing, cross-country skiing, and walking using stationary devices. They found that the energy expended at comparable heart rates is similar no matter what the machine.

80. Don't bother trying to correlate the time of day you train with the time you race. According to a university study, doing so makes no difference to performance.

81. The following ten tips will help you squeeze the most out of your time on an indoor trainer. With some planning, you'll be able to get a good workout in as little as 45 to 60 minutes.

- Warm up efficiently. Five minutes is the minimum; make it 20 if you're going to do a strenuous workout. Afterward, reverse your warm-up procedure to cool down.
- Devise a workout strategy. Don't just ride at one speed each time—you must vary your training to develop speed, power, endurance, and the ability to recover faster.
- Wear a heart rate monitor. This will ensure that you

work intensely enough to improve fitness, not just maintain it.

- Know when to ease off. Include easy or rest days in your schedule to allow your body to recover after hard efforts.
- Keep cool. Always ride with a fan blowing on you to minimize sweating and make it possible to do more work. And don't forget to fill your water bottle.
- Ride to music, not television. TV takes concentration away from the effort, while a hard-driving beat can increase your intensity.
- Focus on your technique. Use a mirror to check your position, and concentrate on applying pressure all the way around the pedal stroke.
- Learn some mental tricks. When doing intervals, for example, don't think about the total number you plan to do. Instead, concentrate on the upcoming one and tell yourself, "One more," so you continue to go hard.
- Pace yourself. Don't start using the indoor trainer too early in the winter or you'll burn out before outdoor riding resumes.
- Go high-tech. Use a computerized trainer that simulates races or obstacles such as hills and headwinds. Or use videotapes that create the illusion of riding outdoors.

82. Use long, intense rides, as well as interval training, to raise your anaerobic threshold (AT). This is your body's breaking point during exercise, the maximum level of riding intensity you can sustain. Before reaching it, most of your energy is produced aerobically (with oxygen). But after exceeding it, a significant amount is produced anaerobically (without oxygen) and you experience breathlessness and muscle discomfort. The higher your AT, the harder you can ride for extended periods.

83. When you return to road riding after a winter of cross-training for aerobic conditioning, increase your strength by doing hill workouts once a week to complement your endurance rides. After warming up, find a gradual hill that's 1 to 2 miles long. Stay seated while climbing and use a gear that allows you to pedal at 60 rpm. As weeks go by,

begin using higher gears that you can still handle at this cadence.

84. One of the best ways to improve is to have a purpose on every ride. If you're cycling with a group, practice your drafting skills by organizing a paceline. On another day, do low-gear sprints to develop your spin, or try hill repeats to improve your climbing. On easy days, work on cornering, no-hands riding, or other skills that won't tax your cardio-vascular system.

85. If you don't have an electronic heart rate monitor, count your pulse manually at the carotid artery in your neck. Find it with your fingertip just beside your Adam's apple. Or you can check the radial artery in your wrist at the base of either thumb.

86. It's not necessarily a waste of time to train below your target heart rate (65 percent of maximum). Sometimes an easy spin is beneficial for muscle recovery and mental refreshment. And if you're out of shape, any riding will bring aerobic improvement.

87. Few things in life are guaranteed, but here's one: If you routinely train in the zone between 65 and 85 percent of your maximum heart rate, you will become fitter.

88. There's no reason to spend hours in the weight room each day during winter training. Six exercises packed into 30 minutes are all you need. Choose an exercise for the quads (squats or leg presses), an upper-body pulling movement such as pull-ups or rows, and a pushing exercise such as dips or bench presses. Then add two "assistance" exercises such as abdominal crunchers and back extensions. Finally, complete each workout with isometric exercises for the neck.

89. Forget toe raises or other exercises to develop the calves. According to experts, during pedaling it's the quadriceps that flex the foot; the calf muscles merely act as a tight wire to transfer the quads' power to the foot and pedal. So instead of doing calf exercises, spend this time developing the strength of your quads.

90. Use cross-training (participating in sports other than cycling) to improve your riding in these four ways.

- Training with weights will isolate and overload certain important muscles, thus developing their strength much better than cycling can.
- Using other sports will reduce the risk of overuse injuries inherent in doing just one activity.
- It will increase overall fitness by conditioning muscles not normally involved in cycling.
- It will reduce the mental staleness that comes from doing the same thing every day. It makes training fun.

91. A simple way to gauge the equivalence of cycling and running is to forget distance and go by time and heart rate. For example, an hour of riding at a certain heart rate is equivalent to an hour of running at the same heart rate. Of course, the body can't tolerate running as well as it can cycling, so you can easily log more time on your bike.

92. If you have a lengthy layoff from training (three months or so), you can get back to within 90 percent of your best in about two months if you do high-quality interval workouts on an indoor trainer, in addition to longer road rides. Try going for five minutes at 90 percent of your maximum heart rate, followed by three minutes of recovery. Repeated four times, this is more effective than a 90-minute ride.

93. Don't become too discouraged if you have an enforced layoff; it might not be as detrimental to your fitness as you'd suspect. Longtime endurance athletes don't exhibit a significant loss of heart function when training is stopped for three months. In addition, such layoffs don't decrease the number of small blood vessels in your muscles—a key fitness factor. However, muscular endurance does decline rather rapidly.

94. Use videotape to evaluate your position and riding style. Enlist a friend or your bike club to share the camera rental, and shoot lots of tape on various terrains. Then analyze it to check all the parameters of correct technique.

3 21 DETAILS THAT WILL IMPROVE YOUR RIDING POSITION

1. To tell if a bike is the correct size for you, stand over it while wearing your riding shoes. For a road bike there should be 1 to 2 inches of clearance between your crotch and the top tube. For a mountain bike, the distance should be 2 to 3 inches so you'll have room to dismount quickly in rough terrain.

2. Compared to a man of the same height, a woman generally needs a bike that measures about 2 centimeters less between the seat tube and head tube.

3. Use this order of adjustments to make a bike of proper size fit your body perfectly: cleat position, saddle tilt, saddle height, knee-over-pedal relationship, reach to handlebar.

4. Toe clips help to maintain proper foot position and increase pedaling efficiency. When the ball of your foot is over the pedal axle, the toe of your shoe should be about ⅛ inch from the end of the clip. This space is necessary to prevent pressure on your toes and damage to the end of your shoes.

5. If your foot size is between toe clip sizes, either use the larger size and have extra room, or select the smaller size and place washers between the clips and the pedals to gain the necessary space.

6. Proper fore/aft alignment of conventional (slotted) shoe cleats is necessary for efficient and injury-free cycling. Basically, cleats should be positioned so that the balls of your feet are directly above the pedal axles. To find the balls of

your feet through rigid-sole cycling shoes, follow these steps.

A. Paint a small white dot on the ball of your bare right foot.
B. Carefully press the foot to the sole of the left shoe (cleat removed) to transfer the paint.
C. Repeat these steps with the left foot and right shoe.
D. Double check by drilling a small hole through the dot on each sole, then putting on the shoes and poking a paint-dipped spoke through the holes. These new dots should appear directly on the ball of each foot.
E. Attach the cleats so when the shoes are engaged with the pedals, the sole holes are over the center of the pedal axles.

7. To adjust the rotational position of conventional shoe cleats, ride a few miles with the cleats loose enough to let your feet find their natural alignment. It's not uncommon for them to be at different angles. Then have a friend reach under and tighten the cleats before you dismount.

8. To check whether your saddle is level or tilted, lay a yard-stick lengthwise on top and see how it relates to the frame's top tube. If your frame has a sloping top tube, set the bike against a bookcase, windowsill, or something else with horizontal lines.

9. It's usually not a good idea to mount your saddle with the nose pointing down even slightly. This can cause arm fatigue as you resist the tendency to slide forward.

10. Try riding no-hands or with very light pressure on the handlebar. If you slide forward, tilt the nose of the saddle up slightly.

11. Saddle height (distance from the top of the saddle to the pedal axle when the crankarm is in line with the seat tube) is not an exact science. Use the following two methods to get into the proper range, then take your body's advice (if any) during rides and make slight refinements.

    • With your bare feet 6 inches apart, hold a tape measure firmly into your crotch and measure to the floor. (Have

a friend help so you're exact.) Multiply this number by
1.09. This number is your saddle height.

- Pedal backward using your heels. Place the saddle just
below the point where you must rock your hips to keep
your feet in contact with the pedal.

12.   Alter your saddle height occasionally if you are still growing
or you ride year-round. It should be lowered in winter in
proportion to the thickness of extra layers of tights and
shorts, or if cold weather tightens your leg muscles.

13.   Use the saddle's fore/aft location to put yourself in the
proper position over the pedals, not to alter your reach to
the handlebar. The latter is accomplished with the stem
extension.

14.   To set the saddle's fore/aft location, follow these steps.

A. Locate your right leg's tibial tuberosity—the bony bump
below the kneecap. This conveniently lies on a vertical
line that passes through the center of the knee joint
when the crankarm is directly forward (3 o'clock). This
line should also bisect the pedal axle.

B. With the bike mounted on a resistance trainer or against
a wall so the top tube is level with the floor, turn the
right crankarm to 3 o'clock and drop a plumb line (a
nut on a string will do) from the front of your tibial
tuberosity.

C. Angle your knee slightly outward, and see where the
string passes the pedal axle. Slide on the saddle until
the string and axle line up, then dismount and move
the saddle accordingly.

15.   Put the top of the handlebar about 1 inch lower than the
top of the saddle. Never position the stem above its min-
imum-insertion mark; 2 inches must remain in the steerer
tube or it could be deformed (and thus weakened) by the
expander plug.

16.   To check for proper stem extension, get on the bike and
assume a normal riding position with hands on the drops
of the handlebar and elbows slightly bent. Have a friend

hold a plumb line to the end of your nose. It should fall about 1 inch behind the bar. If it misses the mark by much, estimate what size the replacement stem should be.

17. After making the necessary adjustments to your position, minor aches and pains may develop before your body adapts to its new riding posture. This is normal, so resist the temptation to keep fiddling. You'll become accustomed to it afer a few rides, and then you can concentrate on bike-handling skills and fitness, confident that your riding position is as good as can be.

18. To facilitate breathing, make sure the width of your handlebar equals the width of your shoulders.

19. The ideal aero bar position places the stem as low as comfort permits, with the forearms parallel to or angled slightly up from the ground. Elbow width should be equal to or less than shoulder width.

20. When installing a full aero handlebar, a shorter, higher stem may be needed to offset quicker handling and oversteer caused by more of your weight being over the front wheel. It will also help maintain proper back position. The new stem should be 1 to 2 centimeters shorter and at least 3 centimeters higher.

21. No stem change should be necessary when attaching a clip-on aero bar. Most models have an adjustable length and raised arm pads.

97 UP-TO-DATE IMPROVEMENTS TO KEEP YOUR BIKE IN SHAPE

1. The two surest and easiest ways to help your bike work well are to maintain proper tire pressure and frequently lubricate your chain.

2. Don't procrastinate when it comes to bike maintenance. If your tire is wearing through or a cable is beginning to fray, replace it now. Otherwise, you risk a breakdown or, worse, an accident.

3. Beware of using a gas station's air pump. It delivers a large volume of air quickly and can blow a bike tire off the rim.

4. Wrap tape around your road bike's seatpost where it enters the frame so you can relocate your ideal saddle height if the post slips or is removed.

5. Memorize or record the distance from the center of your crank axle to the top of the saddle—it's handy when traveling or borrowing a bike.

6. Rotate your tires. The rear tire wears more than twice as fast as the front, so switch them every 1,000 miles to get maximum life.

7. Carry a patch kit and a spare tube, so you're not disabled if you have two flats on a ride.

8. Always carry a spare tube when you plan to ride in the rain. Flats occur more frequently during inclement weather, and it's difficult to apply patches in the rain.

9. Check the glue in your patch kit periodically to be sure it hasn't evaporated.

10. The patches in most clincher tire repair kits have foil on one side and plastic on the other. Remove the foil and place the patch against the tube after you applied the glue. Then pull the plastic off.

11. Use nylon-reinforced strapping tape as a protective rim strip. It's light and thin to aid tire installation and removal, and it doesn't migrate to uncover spoke heads. For narrow rims, cut the tape lengthwise.

12. Build wheels with aluminum alloy nipples. They're as reliable as brass ones and will save a critical ounce per wheel.

13. Write your name, address, phone number, and "this bike was stolen" on a piece of masking tape and stick it to the fork's steerer tube. Then if it ever is, a shop mechanic may someday contact you in the midst of a repair and make your day.

14. If you rip up a 700C clincher tire and the only spare you can get your hands on is a sew-up tire, you *can* use it to ride home on. Be sure to go slow and avoid sharp corners and bumps.

15. Leave some slack in the front derailleur cable. It makes the shift lever easier to grasp since the lever needn't be flush with the down tube when you're using the small chainring.

16. Check tire inflation at least weekly on road bikes and monthly on mountain bikes. Underinflated tires are slower, more prone to wear out, and hazardous since they increase the chance of flats and rim damage.

17. If you develop a problem with your index shifting system during a ride and it has a friction backup, switch to that mode to get home.

18. Align clincher tire's label with the valve stem during installation. Then, if you have a puncture, you can easily locate the corresponding spot on the tire and check for embedded material.

19. Silence annoying clicks and creaks in clipless pedals by

applying a few drops of oil to each shoe's cleat where it contacts the sole and to the pedal-gripping hardware.

20.   Wrap a spare tubular tire in cloth or stow it in a saddle bag to protect its sidewall from damage.

21.   Keep handlebar ends plugged so they won't take a core sample of your thigh in a crash.

22.   Place a section of an old inner tube around the lower race when servicing and reassembling your headset, to keep out dirt and water.

23.   In a pinch, use your toe-strap buckle as a screwdriver.

24.   To (briefly) foil a thief, adjust one brake so when its quick-release is closed it clamps the rim and prevents forward motion. Also, remove or secure your mountain bike's quick-release seat and seatpost when leaving it unattended.

25.   After a crash, it's hard to tell what damage (if any) your bike has suffered. Here's a quick checklist that covers all the major parts. If you suspect a problem, take the bike to a shop mechanic for a more extensive evaluation and re-pairs. Don't risk your safety by riding a damaged bike.

- Frame and fork. Inspect all tube intersections for wrinkles, bulges, and cracks in the paint. These are signs of a bent frame. A straightedge held beside the fork should bisect the head tube of the frame and the fork's top section. Also, an undamaged wheel should sit perfectly centered between the blades. If it is closer to one blade than the other, the fork has been bent.
- Wheels. Spin each one and look for lateral or vertical movement at the rim. Minor hops and wobbles can be removed by truing, but you may need to replace a spoke or even a rim to correct more severe problems.
- Other parts. Look for scratches, dents, and bends on every component. The rear derailleur is susceptible to damage even if the bike merely falls over on its right side, so kneel behind to see if it hangs parallel to the freewheel cogs. (See illustration 4-1.) Carefully check your pedals and brake levers, too. They can also take a beating in a crash.

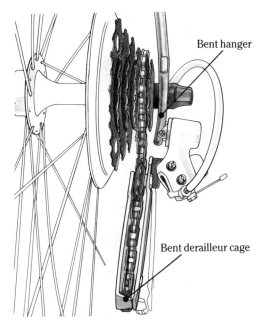

Bent hanger

Bent derailleur cage

Illustration 4-1. Damage checkpoints.

26. Hose down your bike after riding in the rain to remove most of the grit. Then dry it with a towel, and spray a lubricant into the derailleur and brake pivot points and where cables enter or exit their housings.

27. Carry a tire "boot" to repair large cuts. A section of sew-up tire casing about 2 inches long with the tread stripped off is ideal, but a piece of clincher tire, polyurethane tube, or canvas will also work. Place it under the cut, between the tire and tube.

28. Wrap handlebar tape starting from each end and working toward the stem to prevent it from unraveling while riding. Secure the ends near the stem with colored electrical tape.

29. If you frequently bend or break axles, have the alignment of your frame's dropouts checked.

30. If you're using tubular tires and change one on the road because of a flat, help the spare and glue bond by heating

the rim. Do this by riding for a few minutes with the brake lightly applied.

31. For a special, relatively short event such as a time trial, clean all the grease out of your hub bearings and replace it with a light oil. This will reduce friction, but oil quickly leaks out of the bearings, so don't rely on it to perform over an extended period of time.

32. Never use a narrow tire on a wide rim. There isn't enough rubber to protect the metal from potholes and rocks.

33. Check all nuts and bolts on a new bike after the first week of use. If anything is going to loosen, it'll usually happen during the initial miles.

34. Apply an auto wax or one specifically made for bicycle frames to preserve a bike's finish, but keep the wax away from brakes and rims.

35. Always take a new bike back for the free 30-day checkup that most shops offer. (Mark the date on your calendar!) The mechanics are trained to spot and correct slight problems that you may not even notice. After this, your bike shouldn't need professional service for six months to a year, other than chain and cable lubrication.

36. After installing a clincher tire, check to be sure its bead (the thin line molded into the rubber just above the rim) does not bob when the wheel spins. However, don't worry if the line between the tire's tan sidewall and black tread wobbles—most tires have some irregularity and it won't affect performance.

37. If one of your clincher tires loses air more rapidly than the other, its valve may be loose. Check this by inflating the tire to full pressure and putting saliva across the opening. If a bubble slowly forms, have the valve tightened at a bike shop or garage. (This works only for car-type Shrader valves, not European-style Presta.)

38. To touch up nicks and scratches in your bike's paint, first sand the spots bare with 400- or 500-grit sandpaper. Then dab on primer with a small brush, followed by matching paint.

39. If you can't get touch-up paint from the bike's manufacturer, check a toy store for model enamel that's close to the right color. If you're good you can even mix colors to arrive at an exact match.

40. Monitor tire wear on a bald, slick tread by periodically checking the width of the tire's section that contacts the road. As a tire wears, this section becomes wider.

41. Replace your tires if they ever show a fabriclike casing material through their treads. Bulges in the sidewall or tears along the bead line (just above the rim) are also grounds for replacement.

42. You'll know that a quick-release wheel is tight enough in the frame if pushing the lever over leaves an imprint on your palm.

43. To check for a maladjusted headset, stand beside the bike, squeeze the front brake lever, and rock the bike back and forth. A loose headset will be apparent. If it seems okay, check for tightness by slightly elevating the front wheel and letting the handlebar turn from one extreme to the other. If if sticks in either direction, the headset is tight and should be adjusted or repacked.

44. To bring a worn, pitted headset back to life, toss out the bottom race's bearing retainer and install loose balls. Without the retainer, the headset can hold at least one additional bearing and they won't nestle into the same dents.

45. Hang your bike by the wheels if that's the easiest way for you to store it. It won't damage them; in fact, it causes less stress than riding on them.

46. Periodically inspect each tire's tread for embedded glass or other debris. You can often prevent punctures by removing debris before it works through the tire casing.

47. Sometimes a bike seems haunted by mysterious ticks, squeaks, and rattles. Here are their common hiding places and how to silence them.

- When you hear a metallic click during every crank revolution, unscrew each pedal, grease its threads, and retighten it firmly to the crankarm.

- A squeak is from a pedal rather than the chain if it occurs at the same place on each pedal stroke. Spray lubrication on points where the cage and body connect. Also make sure your shoe cleats are on tight. Spray a lubricant between the cleat and sole, then wipe off the excess.
- If the chain chirps, it simply needs lubricating.
- If the chain clicks or jumps, it has a tight link. To find it, kneel at the right side of the bike and turn the crank backward with your hand. Watch the chain as it winds through the rear derailleur pulleys (an inflexible link will be noticeable). Then grasp the chain on either side of the stiff link (use rags to keep your hands clean), bend it laterally to loosen it, and apply lubrication.
- When the handlebar/stem creaks during sprints or climbs, tighten the expander bolt (on top) and binder bolt (in front). If the noise persists, spray a lubricant between the bar and stem.
- Buzzing occurs when a bottle cage, frame pump, or some other add-on part is vibrating. Or it could be a cable housing vibrating against the frame. Touch these things while riding to isolate the problem, then tighten, shorten, reroute, or tape, as necessary.
- Rattles and jingles can come from your tool bag (wrap items with rubber bands or rags), or loose coins in your pocket (try a change purse). If the jingling is caused by a loose dustcap on a hub or the crankset's lockring, give it immediate attention or risk an expensive repair.
- Thumping is usually felt rather than heard. Common causes are dented rims and bulging or improperly seated tires.
- Clicking sounds sometimes come from two spokes rubbing together. Try putting a drop of oil on each spoke crossing.

48.   Don't discard an entire $25 freewheel just because a couple of $4 cogs are excessively worn. In fact, the body of a good-quality freewheel is capable of outlasting several generations of cogs. On the other hand, if you have an old, inexpensive freewheel with several worn cogs, it is wise (and probably less costly) to replace the whole thing rather than install four or five new cogs.

49.   Once high-speed front-end wobble begins, it usually continues until you accelerate, decelerate, or lean hard on the handlebar. It also helps to clamp the top tube between your knees. Among the suspected contributors are a short wheelbase, light wheels, an out-of-true front wheel, loose front axle, pitted or loose headset, flexible frame, long tubes (large frame size), bent fork, misaligned frame, and a riding position that puts insufficient weight on the front wheel.

50.   Don't base your service schedule for hubs on mileage or time. Rather, remove the wheels from your bike monthly (twice a month for mountain bikes ridden off-road) and spin the axle between your thumb and forefinger. Assuming the hub cones are properly adjusted, the axles should turn freely without grinding or binding. If they turn too freely, the grease has probably washed out or dried up. In either case it's time to overhaul the hub.

51.   The axle of a properly adjusted hub should have a hint of looseness to allow for compression when the wheel is fastened to the frame.

52.   When fixing a flat clincher tire, don't reassemble the wheel before carefully feeling around the inside circumference of the tire. Whatever caused the puncture may still be lodged through the tread, ready to strike again.

53.   If a spoke breaks, stop right away and remove it or twist it around its neighbors. A flapping rear-wheel spoke can snag the derailleur and cause significant damage.

54.   Avoid snakebites! Not only the reptilian kind, but those double puncture holes caused by the rim flange pinching the tube when you ride over a rock or other obstacle. An underinflated tire is more likely to bottom out like this, but rider weight is also a factor. If you're heavy, use wider tires and/or add 10 pounds to the maximum pressure listed on the sidewall. Virtually all tires mounted on hook-bead rims can handle it. Slowing down for obstacles also helps.

55.   When the location of a puncture can be easily identified, save time and your spare tube by making the repair this way: Pry about 6 inches of bead from the rim on either side of the leak, and pull out only as much tube as necessary to patch the hole. Then simply reinsert the tube, reseat the bead, and inflate.

56. When transporting your bike by air, reduce tire pressure to about half of normal. Even though baggage compartments are pressurized, this will prevent a blowout in case the level varies, yet it leaves sufficient air to protect tires and rims during handling.

57. If your bike gets immersed in water or caught in a downpour, remove the seatpost and the bottom bracket to allow the moisture in the frame to evaporate quickly, minimizing damage. Placing the frame in a warm place or in the sun will also speed evaporation.

58. If you do a lot of riding in inclement weather, fenders will protect you and your bike frame, plus save on clean-up time and maintenance. Use full-size fenders—the more they cover, the better.

59. If you don't like the mess of cleaning and oiling your chain (and getting the stuff on your clothes and skin), give it the paraffin treatment. It's dry, so it doesn't hold grit. Here's how to do it.

A. Use solvent to remove all oil and grease from the chain and drivetrain. Let the components dry.

B. Melt the wax in a Fry Daddy or other electric deep fryer. (Do this outdoors where it can be watched safely.) Soak the chain in the melted paraffin for at least 10 minutes. Hot paraffin (300°F) penetrates best, but keep it away from open flame and heating coils.

C. Remove and hang the chain so the hot wax can drip off. Allow the chain to cool, then reinstall it. With your bike on a repair stand, spin through the gears to loosen the chain and allow excess wax to flake off.

D. Repeat this procedure every 300 miles or when the chain becomes dirty. There is no need to use solvent for subsequent cleanings because the hot wax will flush away the grit.

60. Rub paraffin wax on the derailleur cables where they pass under the bottom bracket after you loosen and clean them. The wax will provide lubrication, but it won't attract road sludge.

61. Use round rubber ring seals (O-rings), available from hardware stores, to seal out water and grit. They're ideal for:
- Above or within the outermost headset locknut.
- Over the bottom bracket axle, against the fixed cup and adjustable cup. Use several on each side so the innermost rings stay snug against the cups.
- Over the hub locknuts, against the dustcaps.
- Over the pedal axle, against the pedal cage.

62. Pack your hub, pedal, bottom bracket, and headset bearings in heavy, water-resistant grease to withstand wet riding conditions. Good brands are Super Lube and Campagnolo 02-ZPT.

63. Pinch your tires before every ride to make sure there isn't a slow-leaking puncture.

64. Lubricate your chain 24 hours before riding if possible. This will allow the lube's liquid carrier to evaporate and, thereby, keep your drivetrain cleaner since there is no liquid left to attract road dirt.

65. Turn the barrel adjusters counterclockwise to take slack out of cables without tools. These adjusters are found at the point where cable housing connects with the rear derailleur and each brake. (Sometimes they're located atop the brake levers.)

66. Salvage a clincher tire that has a cut sidewall by "booting" the hole. Cut a section of supple casing from an old tire and glue it over the inside of the damage. (Cotton or silk tubular tires make the best boot material, but a section of nylon clincher that has been stripped of tread also works well.) Carefully remount the tire without dislodging the boot.

67. To fix a cut tire in an emergency, fashion a boot from handlebar tape, roadside cardboard—even a piece of an aluminum can. A folded dollar bill works well because it's made of relatively tough linen, not plain paper.

68. Armor-All and similar products will keep your rubber brake lever hoods from drying and cracking. Don't use it on your tires, though, because it makes them slippery and can get on the rims, and interfere with braking.

69. Severe cold won't affect a bike, but avoid subjecting it to extreme changes in temperature or humidity. If you move your bike from a cold garage to a heated house, the temperature change will cause condensation inside the tubes. This will eventually lead to rust.

70. Buy your bike grease in small tubes or containers. A large jar of grease is more likely to become contaminated by dirt. It's also neater to squeeze grease into a bearing race from a tube than having to dip your finger into a jar.

71. Use two different types of greases for the following applications: a smooth, light one for cassette bearings, freewheels, and semisealed bearings (where the O-ring helps keep the grease in place); and a tackier, thicker one for pedals, nonsealed bearings, headsets, and other components where the grease is likely to ooze out and a moisture barrier is needed.

72. Even though nearly all freewheel manufacturers recommend oil, a smooth, light, high-performance grease will do a better job of repelling water and grit.

73. Presta valves often stick closed and don't allow air to fill the tire. The solution is simple. Before inflating a tire, unscrew its valve and fully depress it twice to release a small amount of air. This should free the valve and allow easy inflation.

74. Follow these steps to take the mystery out of tire inflation pressure.
   A. Weigh yourself and your bike together (in pounds) by standing on a scale. This is your total load.
   B. Measure the actual width of one of your inflated tires with a caliper or ruler. Caution: Do not go by the width printed on the sidewall because it may be inaccurate.
   C. Find the diagonal line on the graph (table 4-1) that corresponds to this width (or is closest to it).
   D. Find your total load on the graph's horizontal axis.
   E. Locate the point where your load intersects the line representing your tire width.
   F. Using this point, find your ideal tire inflation pressure on the graph's vertical axis.

TABLE 4-1.

Ideal Inflation Based on Load and Tire Size

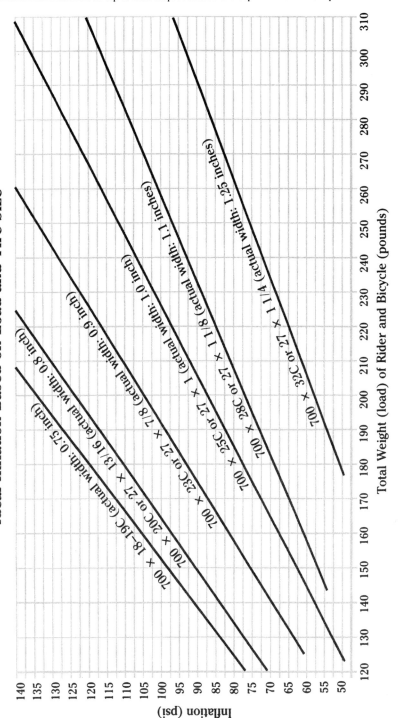

700 × 18-19C (actual width: 0.75 inch)

700 × 20C or 27 × 13/16 (actual width: 0.8 inch)

700 × 23C or 27 × 7/8 (actual width: 0.9 inch)

700 × 25C or 27 × 1 (actual width: 1.0 inch)

700 × 28C or 27 × 1 1/8 (actual width: 1.1 inches)

700 × 32C or 27 × 1 1/4 (actual width: 1.25 inches)

Inflation (psi)

Total Weight (load) of Rider and Bicycle (pounds)

75. Refine your tire inflation pressure to meet special riding needs. For instance, cornering force and shock absorption are increased by decreasing pressure slightly. Such a comfortable, surefooted ride may be desirable for a tour or when riding in the rain. A slightly higher pressure decreases rolling resistance. This is best for a race or time trial where comfort is less important than speed.

76. If you don't have a dishing gauge to determine whether the rim of your wheel is centered between the hub flanges, use your bike's frame. Simply flip the wheel over and check the rim's position relative to the brake pads. Both pads should be identical distances from the rim.

77. To fine-tune the shifting of an index rear derailleur, use the adjustment barrel located where the cable enters the derailleur. Turn the barrel counterclockwise to quicken shifting to larger cogs; turn it clockwise to improve shifting to smaller ones. Adjust it half a turn at a time, then check performance.

78. Put your tire patch kit and other tools in an old tube sock before storing them in your saddle bag. This keeps everything organized and prevents rattling. Then, when you need to make a repair, slip the sock over your hand and arm to keep from getting greasy but still maintain a good grip.

79. Here's a trick for improving the rolling efficiency of a low- to medium-quality hub or bottom bracket. First, disassemble the hub and wipe all parts clean. Then rebuild the unit using Simichrome abrasive metal polishing paste instead of grease. Ride the bike just a few miles so the paste will polish the bearing surfaces. Thoroughly clean the parts and repack with grease and new grade 10 (the finest) ball bearings (use loose balls rather than retainers).

80. To tell if a chain has become worn and stretched measure it with a foot-long ruler. Put the first mark on the center of any rivet, then look at the 12-inch mark. On a new chain it will also be on the center of a rivet. On a worn one, it will fall ⅛ inch or more short of a rivet.

81. Whenever you replace a chain, take a test ride to check for skipping. Push hard in each freewheel cog, staying seated in case what you're looking for actually happens.

Badly worn cogs won't mate with a new chain, so replace the ones that skip.

82. When using a chain tool to remove your chain for cleaning, don't drive the pin out completely because it's very difficult to reinstall. Don't even push the pin so far that the chain falls apart on its own. Drive the pin so that it's flush with the tool's back edge. You should have to bend the chain sideways to separate it.

83. Never use gas to clean your chain or other drivetrain components. It's highly flammable and will strip the parts of all lubrication. Instead, use kerosene or diesel fuel, both of which clean well but leave a light oily film.

84. Discard a chain that has numerous tight links or is stiff with rust.

85. Don't be concerned about the frame flex you notice when you ride your bike on a resistance trainer. Frames are resilient and designed to bend under load. When a bike is immobilized in a trainer, the flex is more apparent than on the road, where it's free to pivot on the tires.

86. Wobbly chainrings can be trued with an adjustable wrench clamped directly on the ring. Carefully adjust the ring by bending it inward or outward as necessary. Do a little at a time and frequently check your progress.

87. If wobbling or noises in the bike's rear hub make you suspect that the axle is broken, do not remove the wheel until you get back home. The quick-release skewer will hold the two axle pieces together and render the bike rideable. But once you remove the wheel, the axle and bearings will fall out.

88. If your wheel develops a wobble, squeeze pairs of spokes to determine if one or more have loosened. If so, simply making them as tight as their neighbors should bring the wheel back into true.

89. There's no danger in keeping your bike mounted on an indoor trainer. The tire might develop a flat spot where is contacts the roller, but this will disappear when it's ridden.

90. Scraping noises from the crank area probably mean the chain is rubbing the front derailleur. This will happen as shifts with the rear derailleur alter the angle of the chain through the cage. To quiet the bike, move the front derailleur lever to center the cage but not cause a shift.

91. Keep in mind when riding and choosing a gear that extreme chain angles, such as when combining the largest rear cog with the large chainring (or smallest cog with the small chainring) may never run quietly or smoothly, which is one reason they shouldn't be used.

92. When setting up a bike repair area in your basement or garage, don't use a pegboard and hooks for hanging your tools. It requires mounting hardware and can limit your tool arrangement. Instead, get a 4×8-foot sheet of $3/4$-inch plywood. Use a large piece of cardboard as a template. Place it on the floor and trace the outline of your tools on it, arranging the most frequently used ones in the center. Place this template against the board, and drive finishing nails in the outlines to support the tools. Remove the template, hang the tools, and trace their outline on the board with a black marker.

93. To make a screwdriver and Allen wrench holder, drill holes in a short 2×4-inch piece of wood and attach it to your tool board.

94. Use a light-colored, stain-resistant indoor/outdoor carpet for your home shop area so it's easy to find small parts if you drop them. Avoid shag rugs and wood floors with cracks.

95. If the chain skips and slips in a certain gear, the problem is a worn freewheel cog. If it happens in all gears, it's caused by a stiff chain link.

96. To solve a disconcerting creak that occurs when climbing in the saddle, try removing the seatpost and greasing the section that goes in the frame.

97. Short Allen keys and poor-fitting wrenches can prevent you from making sufficient tightening and adjustments, while using oversize wrenches can result in overtightening. Always use small tools on small nuts and bolts. If more leverage is required on an Allen key, slip an adjustable wrench or small pipe over its end.

5

37 SPECIFICS FOR MORE EFFECTIVE EQUIPMENT

1. On wet roads, tires with a genuine rubber tread tend to grip better than synthetic types. You can usually see the difference. Synthetics look shiny when new, while a rubber tread is dull. This applies to clinchers, tubulars, and mountain bike tires.

2. Women, particularly those who are short, should consider a specially designed bike. Some companies make models that are built for the female anatomy. A typical woman has a shorter torso and arms, but longer legs, than a man of the same height. She also has narrower shoulders, smaller hands and feet, and a wider pelvis.

3. Avoid using frame-mounted generator lights if you ride in stop-and-go traffic, because they go out as the bike rolls to a halt. Instead, use a light powered by a rechargeable battery pack.

4. Always have at least one rear reflector on your bike for times when you get caught out at dusk. If you ride at night, install a battery-powered red or amber rear light.

5. The best place for reflectors is on the back of your pedals. The up-and-down motion is very effective at catching motorists' attention. If your pedals won't accept bolt-on reflectors, use reflective tape. Put some on your helmet, too.

6. Install a rear rack and pannier, then use your bike for short errands. This keeps you and your car in better shape. The rear bag can carry a tire repair kit, cable lock, and whatever you buy on the trip.

7. So you're buying a new bike? Congratulations! Here are

eight things to check for when you go to the shop to pick it up.

- Make sure it's the exact model, color, and size you want, and that any components were changed or accessories installed as you ordered.
- Wear your riding clothes and shoes so it's easy to accurately adjust the seat and handlebar.
- Spin the wheels to make sure they're true and the brakes don't rub.
- Verify that the tires are inflated to the manufacturer's recommended pressure.
- Find out how the quick-release hubs work. If you're uncertain, then remove and reinstall a wheel several times to become familiar with the procedure.
- Learn how to remove slack from the gear and brake cables using the barrel adjusters.
- Before heading for home, go for a short test ride to make sure the brakes and derailleurs are working properly.
- Don't forget the owner's manual, then read it thoroughly prior to your first real ride.

8. If your present saddle is a pain in the, uh ... a source of discomfort, replace it with one that contains extradense foam padding or gel. These conform to the body while providing necessary support.

9. In choosing a saddle, the key factor is the distance between your "sit bones." These should be your contact points with the saddle top. Because many women have a wider distance than men between these bones, they can find more comfort on saddles that are designed for their anatomy.

10. Use these equipment tips when riding in rainy weather.

- Wear bright yellow or orange to be visible to motorists.
- Put a visor or cap under your helmet to shield your eyes.
- Install lightweight plastic or aluminum fenders, which keep dirty road water off you and your bike surprisingly well.
- Keep your frame waxed and drivetrain well lubricated.

- Use wide, slightly underinflated tires to increase contact with the road.
- Service your bike immediately upon reaching your destination. Hose it off, wipe it down with a towel, then lubricate the chain and use a water-dispersing spray, such as WD-40, on all cables, housings, and the pivot points of the brake and gear systems.

11. U-locks are the favored type because they're easy to carry and hard to violate. But whatever type lock you choose, always use it—a thief can be gone with your bike in seconds. Lock the frame and both wheels to a fixed object, making sure the bike can't simply be lifted over it.

12. Just as your body needs to be specially outfitted for winter riding, so does your bike. Mudguards deflect slush that soaks clothing and fouls the drivetrain and brakes. Lightweight models are available for most bikes.

13. A helmet-mounted rearview mirror is one of the most effective pieces of protective equipment a cyclist can use. It allows you to see what's behind without turning your head and shoulders, a potentially hazardous maneuver.

14. To make your bicycle more aerodynamic, smooth its surfaces of holes, gaps, and protrusions. A rough or uneven surface traps air, and produces a drag. Quick-release levers, screws, bolts, clamps, sharp corners, etc., all contribute to this type of drag.

15. When a race course is wet, put a better tire on the front wheel and corner until the rear one slips a little. Then you'll know the limits of traction. This works because a small skid with the rear tire can be controlled, while if the front breaks traction you'll lose steering control.

16. Clean all leather accessories regularly (except gloves and chamois) to prevent damage from road grit and dryness. Use a soft, damp cloth and saddle soap or leather cleaner, rubbing the item with a circular motion until there's plenty of lather. Wipe away the residue with another clean, damp cloth and buff with a dry rag. Then apply a conditioner, and use a waterproofing agent if you do much riding in foul weather.

17. It's best to have two air pumps: a floor model for home use and a frame-mounted one for emergencies. A frame pump won't last long if used every day, so save it for times when you have no other option.

18. If the head of your floor pump blows off the valve stem, hold it with your foot. Another solution is to cut a slot in the middle of a section of old inner tube, making it just large enough for the head to fit through. Then place the head over the valve, wrap the ends of the tube over the tire, tie them in place, and pump.

19. Use grease, not oil, to relubricate the plunger's cupped washer inside a pump. Oil will get inside the inner tube and rot the rubber.

20. To prevent a frame pump from backfiring, place the head onto the valve just far enough to adequately grip it. Pushing it too far will depress the valve, release the high pressure, and cause the pump handle to shoot back suddenly, striking you and/or breaking the pump.

21. If you're riding on smooth-tread tires and the rear one slips on climbs, try substituting a treaded model. But a better—and less costly—solution is to shift your weight rearward when climbing, like mountain bikers do.

22. If your bike doesn't have "click" shifting and you want to install it, realize that index components work best as "systems." Use the same brand and model of shift lever, freewheel, rear derailleur, chain, cable, and housing. If you mix and match, there's no guarantee that shifting will be reliable.

23. Installing a fairing—a windshield—on your bike will help its aerodynamics, and here's another advantage: In winter, it protects you from the frigid wind.

24. Tires with a Kevlar bead can easily be folded for carrying, but don't try it with a steel-bead tire. The metal will develop a kink that may result in a sidewall blowout.

25. Installing lighter inner tubes is one of the most economical ways to improve performance. This is because wheel weight has a profound effect on acceleration and speed, and premium tubes weigh about two ounces less than standard ones. Yet they cost only about $2 more—a bargain compared with paring wheel weight by replacing tires, rims, or spokes.

26. Compared to aluminum alloy rims, chromed steel rims give poor braking in wet weather and are not recommended. They're also heavy and not inherently stronger.

27. When shopping for a rechargeable lighting system, be aware that there are two types of batteries. Gel cells, like those used in automobiles, are less expensive than nickel-cadmium batteries should you need to replace one, but they require more care. They must not be drained, which damages them and reduces their life. They also can die if unused for long periods. Nickel-cadmium batteries, on the other hand, thrive on "deep cycling" (exhausting and recharging). You can't ruin them by overuse, so their life span is longer than that of gel cells. They're also smaller and lighter. Their disadvantage is that they lose power rapidly at the end of their charge, so you can find yourself abruptly without light.

28. Consider a helmet-mounted headlight if you ride on trails or roads that require a lot of turning. Looking toward the inside of a corner fills the area with light. Another advantage is its ability to track an object. It's also handy for making emergency repairs. Disadvantages include glare when riding in drizzle or fog, more weight on the head, and a chance that the helmet's protective qualities may be compromised in a crash.

29. To determine whether your bike can accept fenders, just hold them in place. The most likely locations for interference are at the fork crown and brake bridge (the small tube that joins the seatstays and supports the rear brake). If the tire rubs regardless of how you position the fenders, your bike wasn't made for them.

30. If your frame has enough clearance for fenders but lacks the dropout eyelets for attaching them, buy a pair of Blackburn custom eyelets to attach the rear one, and use Blackburn stay clamps on the fork to attach the front.

31. If your floor pump is a few years old, beware of what the built-in pressure gauge tells you. In most cases, old pumps read low by as much as 20 psi, which contributes to underinflation and snakebite flats.

32. To prevent your glasses from fogging, smear both sides of the lenses with a little gel toothpaste and rinse with cold water. Then gently towel dry.

33. If you intend to buy a "hybrid" bike (combination road and mountain bike), base its size on your intended use. If you're going to ride primarily on pavement, use your road bike size because crotch clearance isn't an issue since you don't need to dismount quickly and often, and the longer top tube will put you in a more efficient position. If you plan to use your bike for both road and off-road riding, use a frame a couple of inches smaller than your road size, both for improved crotch clearance and to move the handlebar closer for control on steep descents.

34. Never ride on the road with earphones. Although music is a great motivator, it's also an excellent source of distraction, which compromises your safety in traffic. Besides, cycling with earphones is illegal in a number of states.

35. Looking for a quicker, easier way to install and remove your handlebar-mounted heart rate monitor? Take off its wristwatch-style strap and replace it with one of those Velcro models often used to secure frame-mounted pumps. Then you can strap the monitor to the bar without needing a bulky piece of foam to make it fit.

36. Grease the quick-release and mounting bolt threads on your automobile rack to prevent freezing or breakage due to rust.

37. Memorize your gear ratios or write them down on a small card and tape it to the handlebar next to the stem. Why? So you can relate to articles that deal with gear ratios, and so you can select freewheels with cog sizes just right for your needs.

6 45 IMPROVEMENTS FOR THE MOUNTAIN BIKER

1. To save valuable time in a mountain bike race, drill an extra valve hole in your rim and insert a second, uninflated tube in the tire. If the first tube goes flat, you can simply inflate the second.

2. When riding over terrain that requires frequent portages, carry as much of your gear as possible on your body. Use a fanny pack if necessary.

3. Pay careful attention to the condition of your brake pads, and replace them regularly. They wear out quickly and become misaligned, especially in sand or mud. Neglected brakes can hit the tire or the spokes, damage your equipment, and risk your safety.

4. Use rubbing alcohol to install stubborn handlebar grips. It's a lubricant that evaporates quickly, and leaves the grips secure.

5. Install your frame pump behind the seat tube, if possible. This frees the main triangle for accessories.

6. Put a knobbier, wider tire on the front wheel to keep it from sliding out in corners.

7. Opt for a smaller frame if you're unsure about the exact size to ride. More top-tube clearance can't hurt when you have to hop off to prevent a fall.

8. Contrary to popular belief, all mountain bike tires, from skinny models for road riding to the fattest knobbies, will fit on all mountain bike rims. In fact, using fat tires on

narrow rims makes the tire profile more round and thus increases flotation and rim protection.

9. Clean your mountain bike frequently—this is the most important rule of maintenance. Dirt acts as a grinding compound when it gets between moving parts, so hose down the bike after every ride, especially if you've been riding in muddy or sandy conditions.

10. If you're careful, you can clean your bike at a self-serve car wash. Just don't let the high-pressure wand blast water into the bearings of the headset, crankset, or hubs.

11. Never ride with the crankset completely submerged. The flexing from pedaling will let water through the bearing seals.

12. Get better traction on off-road terrain by following these four fundamentals.

   - Prepare your equipment. Adjust tire pressure in accordance with your weight, riding style, and surface conditions. In most cases it should range between 20 and 40 psi.
   - Stand up. This enables you to use the strength of your upper body to dynamically pulse the rear tire. This is done by bending your elbows, lowering your head toward the stem, and pulling back and up on the handlebar at the beginning of each pedal stroke.
   - Read the surface. Frequently glance farther ahead than normal to spot loose gravel, ruts, rock slabs, downed limbs, and the like, so you can more easily overcome the obstacles by using a different line or speed. Plotting a course in this way eliminates the need for abrupt changes in direction—a big benefit since turning wastes traction that could otherwise be used for forward drive.
   - Maintain your speed. Shift to the proper gear ahead of time and hit each tricky section with as much momentum as is reasonable and controllable. Once you're in the bad stuff, accelerate some more and keep your front wheel light to reduce the chance of digging in.

13. To get better performance in conditions where tire grip is key, particularly climbs on a loose surface, ride a bike with

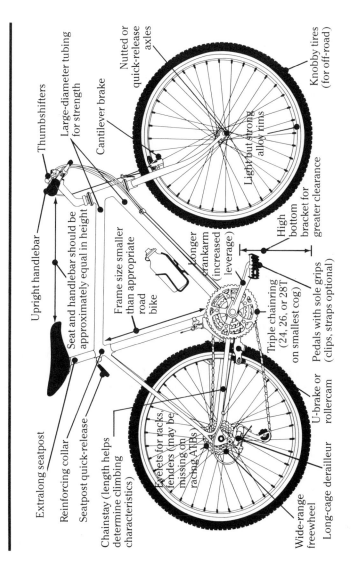

Thumbshifters

Large-diameter tubing for strength

Nutted or quick-release axles

Cantilever brake

Knobby tires (for off-road)

Upright handlebar

Light but strong alloy rims

Seat and handlebar should be approximately equal in height

Frame size smaller than appropriate road bike

Longer crankarm (increased leverage)

High bottom bracket for greater clearance

Triple chainring (24, 26, or 28T on smallest cog)

Pedals with sole grips (clips, straps optional)

Extralong seatpost

Reinforcing collar

Seatpost quick-release

Chainstay (length helps determine climbing characteristics)

Eyelets for racks, fenders (may be missing on racing ATBs)

U-brake or rollercam

Wide-range freewheel

Long-cage derailleur

Illustration 6-1. Anatomy of a mountain bike.

short chainstays. Generally, if you're shorter than 6 feet, look for chainstays of 17.25 inches or less. If you're taller, you will do fine on slightly longer ones.

14. Look for changes in ground color. In dry climates, for instance, darker soil usually harbors more moisture and better traction.

15. Improve your climbing ability with these tips from champion off-road rider John Tomac.

   • Shift your weight to maintain traction. If the rear tire starts to slip on a climb, remain seated and slide back on the saddle. Conversely, if the slope is so steep that the front wheel lifts off the ground, lean forward and slide toward the nose of the saddle.
   • Pick a line. Look at least 10 yards up the trail and choose a course that snakes around potential momentum stoppers such as rocks, ruts, and logs.
   • Anticipate downshifts. If you have already shifted to a lower gear before a steep climb, you won't lose momentum. Also be sure you are in the correct chainring, as it's more difficult to shift to a smaller ring than a larger freewheel cog under pedaling pressure.
   • Find your optimum saddle height. Your saddle should be positioned so that your knee is slightly bent when your foot is at the bottom of the pedal stroke. Too low or too high steals power and control.
   • Stay easy on the grips. Don't even wrap your thumbs around the grips unless it's necessary for control. This will minimize hand and arm fatigue.
   • Spin a bigger gear at a lower cadence. A lower gear will deliver smooth power and permit you to easily lift your weight off the saddle to float over obstacles.
   • Stay in the saddle. Try to spend most of your time in the saddle, because this position affords optimum weight distribution and traction.

16. If your bike has an upturned handlebar, angle the rising portion slightly back toward you.

17. You can position a flat handlebar several ways, depending on terrain and riding style. The most common position is with the bend turned toward you and tipped up slightly.

But feel free to alter this to get a position that feels natur .
and comfortable.

18. If you're considering reducing the width of your handlebar
by cutting off its ends, first experiment with the narrower
width by moving the grips and levers inward.

19. Find the best brake lever position by loosening the levers
enough so they can be moved. Then sit in the saddle, and
place the levers at an angle that doesn't require bending
your wrists up or down. Keep in mind that bent wrists
hinder braking ability, and a severe bump could make you
lose your grip.

20. Brake lever tips shouldn't extend beyond the end of the
handlebar because they'll be damaged if the bike falls over.

21. Don't brake too much on technical descents. Obviously,
you don't want to go too fast and lose control, but you need
momentum to power the bike over logs, rocks, and other
obstacles. Plus, the faster a wheel is spinning, the greater
its resistance to tipping over.

22. When applying the brakes, use them both but apply the
front more firmly—especially on descents, since there is
more weight on the front tire.

23. Lighten up on the rear brake if the rear wheel begins to
skid. A turning wheel has more control than a skidding
wheel.

24. Use these tips when what lies ahead is a boggy mess of
mud.

- Prepare yourself by braking before the wallow. Shift to
  a lower gear (lowest if it looks really deep), and slide
  back on the saddle so you won't go over the handlebar.
- Momentum is the key. Stay in the saddle and keep
  pedaling to maintain balance and forward progress. Use
  the straightest line, because turning steals momentum.
- Go through puddles rather than around them. Standing
  water usually indicates firmer, less permeable soil.
- Pedal smoothly. If you're light, perhaps your tires won't
  sink and you can "float" through. But if you're heavy,
  you'll sink to the bottom and have to power and churn.

● Take downhill mudholes in the middle chainring. If you relax and ride smoothly, you may carry enough momentum to ride through easily.

25. Be responsible when riding in muddy conditions. The path you choose can affect natural landscapes and even the environment. In particular, don't ride muddy slopes that end in streams or ponds. The tire tracks you leave behind form sluiceways that encourage soil erosion.

26. Ride straight through the middle of a mudhole. It is the least damaging route. If each person skirts the edge, for instance, the mudhole will grow until it's wider than it is long.

27. Coat your bike's chain with a thick, gooey lubricant to protect it in wet, muddy conditions. This will help keep most of the mud out of the moving parts. Coat the entire drivetrain with a nonstick vegetable cooking spray.

28. "Chain suck" occurs when the chain catches on the trailing edge of the smallest chainring's teeth and gets wedged between the ring and the chainstay. To prevent it, keep the parts lubricated and in good condition.

29. When you hear the disconcerting "scrunch" of chain suck and it feels as if a stick has been jammed through your chainrings, stop pedaling immediately. Either get off and turn the crank backward to free the chain, or learn to do it with your feet while on the fly. Otherwise, you risk damage to the chain, chainring, and chainstay.

30. Check for a maladjusted headset by standing beside the bike, firmly applying the front brake only, and rocking the bike back and forth. Play or clunking sounds mean the headset is loose. If it seems okay, grasp the top tube, lift the front wheel several inches, and see if the handlebar will turn freely and fully from side to side. If it sticks, the headset is too tight.

31. Check your valve stems regularly to make sure they're still perpendicular to the rim, especially when using low tire pressure. Low pressure can cause the rim to spin inside the tire and tear the valve from the tube. If you see this happening, deflate the tube and realign it.

32. Early in the season, stuff a pruning saw that safely folds up or a small garden hand rake into your fanny pack every time you go trail riding. Stopping to clear or repair a section takes just moments and it'll make a better trail you can enjoy throughout the summer.

33. Perform these wheel checks once a week to make sure a failure doesn't leave you stranded on the trail.

- Overinflate your tires by 10 psi. If the brake pads have worn the rim excessively, they will fold and/or crack under this pressure. If the rim holds, return the tire to normal inflation for riding.
- Check the rim's spoke holes for telltale bulges or cracks. These are warnings that spoke nipples are beginning to pull through. At this point, it's necessary to replace the rim.
- Give each spoke a wiggle. Tighten any loose ones with a spoke wrench until they're as tight as their same-side neighbors.

34. Uneven spoke tension and/or excessive lateral force from sliding or impact is what causes a rim to assume the uneven shape of a potato chip. To make the wheel straight enough to ride back home, do this:

- Remove the wheel. Hold it so the sections that curve inward are at the top and bottom. Hold the sections that curve outward in each hand. Place the top of the wheel against a solid unmovable object and rest the bottom on the ground. Brace the bottom with your foot and push the sides with both hands until the tire resumes its proper shape. (See photograph 6-1.) Repeat if necessary.
- Reinstall the wheel and use a spoke wrench to true it between the brake pads. Shoot for clearance, not perfection.

Photograph 6-1. Straightening a wheel.

35. Even though freehubs need minimal maintenance and they have no oil ports or grease fittings, repack the axle bearings annually, or more often if you ride in the crud. Keep in mind that some of the grease you use will find its way into the freehub bearings.

36. Always carry these handy items.

- Small locking pliers. They can serve as an adjustable wrench, spoke wrench, cable and spoke cutter, or clamp to hold together broken parts.
- Zip ties. They're strong enough for emergency component repairs.

- Nylon-reinforced strapping tape. Use several layers in place of normal rim strips and then you can remove some to boot a tire or secure loose parts.
- Pocketknife, preferably one with all the bells and whistles.
- Drilled-through cable anchor bolt. Any bike shop can sell you one. Then if you lose or strip a brake or derailleur cable fixing bolt, you can improvise a repair.

37. Check your hubs once a week or after your bike dries following every wet ride. Remove the wheels and turn each axle between your thumb and forefinger. The action should be smooth, not gritty. You should feel a slight drag as the bearings roll through the grease. If the action is crunchy or the axle spins too freely, it's time for cleaning and repacking.

38. Just because your bike may have "sealed" hubs doesn't mean dirt and water can't get into the bearings. Cleaning and regreasing is still necessary and can be done on most hubs after the rubber seal is carefully lifted away with an X-acto knife.

39. Lighten your bike and improve comfort by installing a high-tech handlebar made of lightweight steel, aluminum, titanium, or a composite material. Just as a light-gauge frame rides smoother than one with stouter tubes, a thin-wall handlebar transmits less shock to your hands, arms, and shoulders than a heavier model of the same material.

40. Always obey the International Mountain Bicycling Association's "Rules of the Trail."
- Ride on open trails only.
- Leave no trace.
- Control your bicycle.
- Always yield to hikers.
- Never spook animals.
- Plan ahead.

41. When cycling in the desert, never stray off-trail and ride over the thin layer of vegetation called cryptogamic crust.

This ground cover (known as the "glue of the desert") is a community of moss, lichen, microfungi, and cyanobacteria. Once this crust is crushed by bike tires, the underlying sand blows over neighboring cryptogams, blocking their light and air. And when it rains, tire tracks start a miniature gully system that will continue to grow larger because of erosion.

42.   To loft the front wheel over a bump or object, simultaneously lower your torso, apply a hard pedal stroke, and lift with your arms. You'll stay in balance and, by shifting weight forward a bit, the rear wheel will be free to bounce over lightly.

43.   The rougher the trail, the more important it is to relax your body and let your bike do its own thing. Think of your arms and legs as a highly sophisticated and efficient independent suspension system that enables your body to float over the ground.

44.   The farther you ride into the backcountry (and thus the farther you get from civilization), the greater your need to ride responsibly. It's not only a question of personal safety. If you become incapacitated in the outback, others will also risk their safety to go in and rescue you.

45.   Never quit trying. To progress as a mountain biker, you must try to ride everything. Think of it as the Wile E. Coyote technique for cycling excellence. After an unsuccessful attempt, get up, dust yourself off, think about what just happened, then turn around and try it again. If you still don't succeed, leave it for another day. The trail will always be there waiting for you, just like the Road Runner. You see, that bird isn't defeating the coyote; he's only helping him reach for a higher level of creativity. That's how to look at those nasty trail sections that always give you fits. They're there to help you improve.

20 TIME-TESTED TIPS FOR FASTER RACES AND CENTURIES

1. For information about organized road or off-road competition, contact the U.S. Cycling Federation, 1750 E. Boulder St., Colorado Springs, CO 80909. The USCF is the national governing body for amateur racing. It can send you a license application and the name of its representative and member clubs in your locale.

2. Try some club time trials and criteriums before entering USCF events. The time trials will help you gauge your speed, while the crits will furnish important bike-handling and tactical lessons.

3. Before a race, crumple your paper number and attach it to your jersey with extra pins. This keeps it from billowing while you ride.

4. To add at least 1 mph to your average speed in a time trial, install an aero handlebar.

5. Never draft a rider with a torn jersey or shorts, or road rash. These telltale signs mean that he crashed, and he and his bike may not be in the best shape.

6. Always wear a T-shirt under your racing jersey. The garments will slide against each other in a crash and help protect you from road rash.

7. When you need to gain an extra mile per hour during a sprint, tell yourself to pedal "faster," not "harder." The latter will only tense your muscles and increase your mental strain.

8. "A lot of people forget about mental preparation," cautions

veteran racer Ian Jackson. "They think it's all training and they just go out and pound away. But I feel that 50 percent of my success is from mental preparation and the knowledge of what goes on within a race. I'm not one of the strongest riders, I'm not one of the quickest, but race smartness has helped me a great deal."

9.   "Don't work on your bike the day before the event," advises former U.S. pro champ Thomas Prehn. By then it should be completely tuned and road tested. "I've seen guys do a big overhaul the night before an event, then forget to tighten something when they put it back together. During the race, it starts to fall off." Also, "Psychologically, I don't think you should be messing with your bike the day before an event. You should just relax."

10.   You must know where to "pour on the coals" in order to reach the finish line at top speed. Before a race, pedal back from the line in your sprinting gear and count pedal revolutions. After about 40 your top speed starts to deteriorate, so when you reach this number, note a landmark. This is the place to begin your finishing sprint. Then you'll be certain that if anyone gets past you it's for only one reason: they're faster. If you wait longer to start your sprint, you won't be able to reach and sustain top speed. If you start sooner, you'll be cooked before the line.

11.   To maximize your endurance during a long event such as a century, follow these guidelines.

- Drink before you're thirsty, and consume as much as two bottles of water per hour on a warm day.
- Eat carbohydrate-rich meals (pasta, rice, potatoes, etc.) during the three days before the event. Have fruit, oatmeal, cereal, and bread for breakfast.
- During the ride, eat before you're hungry. Bananas, dried fruit, dates, cookies, and commercial energy bars are excellent choices.
- Eat lightly but steadily. Stuff your pockets at rest stops, not your stomach.
- Vary your riding position. Move your hands from the drops to the brake lever hoods to the top of the han-

dlebar. Stand on the pedals and arch your back for relief from bent-over cycling. Do slow neck rolls and shoulder shrugs to prevent upper-body stiffness.

- Divide the ride into segments and have a strategy for each.
- Make sure your bike is properly geared for the course. For advice, ask the ride organizer or someone who has ridden there before.
- Wear cycling shoes that fit comfortably, cycling shorts with a chamois, and cycling gloves. Also wear sunglasses to protect your eyes and reduce fatigue from glare.
- Ride with a friend who has a similar pace or time goal. The companionship and conversation will help the miles pass more quickly.
- If fatigue sets in, don't dwell on the remaining miles. Instead, concentrate on form, efficiency of motion, and drinking and eating adequately. Rest if necessary, but don't stay off the bike for more than 10 minutes.

12. Time trials are a great way to try out organized racing because they're safe—it's just you and your bike against the clock. Here are some tips from 1984 Olympic road champion Connie Carpenter Phinney.

- Avoid risking mechanical failure by double-checking everything and practicing on new equipment before the event.
- Don't be discouraged if you lack the latest technology. Simply lower your stem 1 to 2 centimeters to encourage a streamlined position, keep your elbows close to your body, your head down, and your eyes up.
- Discipline yourself to ride at a cadence of at least 90 rpm. Good form and a brisk cadence are the keys to speed.
- To get good results, you must do specific workouts. Twice a week, ride slightly above your desired time trial speed for a given distance or time.
- Keep a positive mental attitude. Time trials can hurt, and they give you lots of time to think about it. But your preparation can minimize the pain and pay off frequently in personal best performances.

13. Most novice racers make the same mistakes—errors in judgment and technique that result in their frustration, sub-par performance, and burnout. Here is a list of the most common mistakes and how to avoid them.

- Trying to be what you're not. Learn which events to emphasize and which to avoid based on your body type, temperament, and training time.
- Not setting goals. Set daily, weekly, monthly, and season-long objectives, and train for events that mean the most to you.
- Going it alone. The most important thing a new racer can do is find a knowledgeable rider, train with him or her, and ask questions. If no such rider is available, attend a training camp.
- Being impatient. Approach your competitive career as a long-term commitment, realizing that it may take as much as a decade to get your best results.
- Training too hard. Training hard is the only way to improve, but it's important to rest well, too. Do at least two rides per week when your heart rate doesn't go above 120 beats per minute.
- Overemphasizing equipment. Have a decent bike with a good drivetrain and reliable wheels, but remember that you're competing against other riders, not other bicycles.
- Failing to learn from strengths and weaknesses. Train to improve your weak points, and race to use your strong ones.
- Not having a race strategy. Don't adopt a wait-and-see attitude. Devise a game plan that reflects your talents, then stick by it—refine the plan but never abandon it.
- Using wrong gearing for hilly courses. Don't trust the advice of others, because strength and climbing styles differ. Try to ride or drive the course beforehand.
- Being unprepared for wet weather. Train in the rain occasionally so you'll know what to expect.
- Quitting. Many new riders don't realize how hard racing is, but dropping out should never be an option. The more you suffer in a race, the greater your chances of doing well.

14. Don't drive a long way to a race without allowing adequate time for a warm-up. Legs can become stiff when confined to a car for hours.

15. If you want to be part of the race, stay in the front third of the pack. Any farther back and you lose the ability to have a say in the action.

16. If you're like most entry-level racers, who begin by riding criteriums, work on your cornering so the events aren't so difficult. One way to do this is to find a square block (like a criterium course) and practice pedaling through the turns, accelerating out of the corners, and holding a certain speed for two or more laps.

17. Here are eight points to remember for successful criterium racing.

- Don't get discouraged. Because of factors such as drafting, luck, and position in the pack at crucial moments, the strongest rider doesn't always win. In fact, most riders serve a lengthy apprenticeship before doing well. You should never let a poor initial performance get you down.
- Don't quit. At some point in nearly every race, you're going to want out. No matter how much it hurts, try to fight through the bad times. However, if every race is a struggle, examine your training methods.
- Maintain a good position in the pack. It's easier (and safer) to stay at the front than to ride at the back and try to move up.
- Be prepared to ride hard from the start. In most criteriums the initial laps are blazing. Warm up thoroughly and get a starting position in the first few rows. Do whatever it takes to stay with the pack early on, realizing that the pace will ease in time.
- Know how to corner safely. Stay relaxed with your elbows flexed, so when someone bumps you, you don't lose control. Get confident by riding the corners fast during the warm-up. In the race, instead of focusing on the rider in front of you, look at least four or five riders down the road so you can spot danger in time to react.
- Race smart. It's after the halfway point that the racing

really begins. Because early attacks and breakaways rarely succeed, be careful about using your energy to join them. Also, try to notice which riders have poor bike-handling skills or bikes with mechanical problems, such as worn tires, and stay away from them.

- Always finish strong. Usually there's an attack with a kilometer to go, a counterattack 500 meters from the line, and the sprint starts with 250 meters left. You must always be ready to jump. If you aren't a strong sprinter but can sustain a good burst, try a short solo break. If you can get a gap, you might just make it stick.

- Develop all your abilities. Experiment with different tactics because that's the way you'll improve. It's a truism in racing that in order to win, you have to risk losing.

18. To improve your time trial performance, use a heart rate monitor. By knowing your exact pulse during an event, you can maintain maximum energy output, and eliminate mid-race lapses in concentration.

19. Think of a time trial as the interplay between two absolutes and one variable. The absolutes are your most efficient heart rate and a cadence of about 90 rpm. The variable is gearing. Choose a gear ratio that enables you to maintain optimal heart rate and cadence.

20. When time trialing, pay strict attention to your form. Even small changes in body position profoundly affect air drag by increasing frontal area. These include such movements as turning your head to the side, sitting up, or reaching down to shift gears.

57 HINTS FOR LONG-DISTANCE TOURING

1. To receive free maps for a tour, as well as excellent brochures on accommodations, attractions, climate, and history, contact the tourism office of the state you'll be visiting and the chambers of commerce in the towns you'll be riding through.

2. On tours that will take you to remote locations far from bike shops, carry emergency spokes made by cutting the heads off extralong spokes and putting two 90-degree bends at each end. These can be installed without removing the freewheel.

3. Always carry a rivet extractor for installing or removing the chain. It's almost impossible to improvise when you don't have one, and it's small, light, and inexpensive.

4. On a group tour, take a car or van and have riders alternate as the "sag wagon" driver. Or, have a noncycling friend or family member drive. This allows you to travel light and take a rest day if needed.

5. Try to reach your destination by midday. Then, remove your panniers and explore the area unencumbered or go for a fast ride.

6. Travel light. It's not uncommon to unpack after a trip and discover several "indispensable" items that were never touched.

7. You don't need a complete wardrobe, even on an extended tour. Make the most of what you're wearing when you start, and carry a change of underwear, socks, and a shirt. Choose clothes that you can wash and dry quickly.

8. Always pack rain gear. (It's the best way to make sure it won't rain.)

9. Check your list, then check it again. Cross off anything that's unnecessary. You want to be comfortable, and a large part of that comfort will be determined by the amount of weight you carry.

10. Pack heavy items and things you don't use frequently, such as tools, in the bottom of your panniers to keep the center of gravity low. Then pack the rest of your spare items.

11. For optimum bike handling with loads of 20 pounds or more, put approximately 60 percent of the cargo in the rear panniers, 35 percent in the front panniers, and 5 percent in a handlebar bag. Balance the load from side to side to ensure a stable ride at all speeds.

12. Front panniers, which are usually one-third smaller than rear ones, are best mounted on a low-riding rack that centers them with the front axle. The farther away from the axle the front load is carried, the more difficult steering becomes.

13. Put a heavy item that should be accessible, such as a telephoto camera lens, in the top of a low-riding front pannier.

14. Roll your clothes and they'll take less space. Put them in see-through plastic bags to keep them clean, dry, and organized.

15. If you take a cooking kit, use the pot to hold your spices, scouring pads, and other small items. To save space, remove food from bulky packages and put it into plastic bags.

16. Put your most frequently used items in your handlebar bag. For example, your camera, notebook, map, and tire repair kit.

17. Never start a tour with full bags. If you've squeezed all your

gear into the panniers and strained the zippers shut, what happens the first time you stop to buy local artifacts or a bag of cookies? There will always be things added to your belongings as the adventure progresses.

18. Reserve one rear pannier for soiled items such as a tent, groundcloth, and shoes. Similarly, wet items should be kept from dry ones.

19. Panniers that provide external mesh side pockets are great for drying bathing suits, towels, and laundry as you roll down the highway.

20. Pack the most bulky items, such as a sleeping bag and pad, atop the rear rack.

21. Although some panniers are made of waterproof material, don't take chances. Put everything you pack into sturdy plastic bags with tight closures.

22. The trick to mounting, dismounting, and walking a loaded touring bike is to keep it vertical so its weight stays centered over the wheels. Otherwise, it'll take lots of strength to keep it from tumbling over.

23. To get good photos on a tour, develop the mental discipline to look for good picture possibilities. By keeping your camera ready—atop the contents of your handlebar bag or at your side with the strap across your neck and shoulder—you will greatly improve your chances of capturing memories the way no other medium can.

24. Consider using one of the new recyclable cameras. After taking 24 pictures, you simply give the entire package to a photo developer. Some models are even waterproof, making them ideal for bike touring.

25. When you're about to shoot a picture, stop and ask yourself, "What's the subject of the photo I'm taking?" Once you have the answer, try to eliminate extraneous matter from the picture. This takes self-discipline and practice.

26. To save weight on a long tour and prevent rolls of exposed film from being damaged or lost, mail them to a photo developer back home and arrange for future pickup.

27. Although every ounce added to your pack means there's more to carry, don't deprive yourself of a few simple luxuries. For example, use stainless steel pots instead of aluminum, which don't heat as evenly and are harder to clean. Take some spices to add flavor to bland camp food. Pack your favorite slippers and a small pillow for more comfort at campside.

28. American Youth Hostels (AYH) is a national nonprofit organization that provides its members with inexpensive accommodations (often $4 to $12 per night). At last count, there were 275 AYH facilities in 42 states. For information, contact AYH National Office, Box 37613, Washington, DC 20013-7613.

29. Going overseas? AYH can also supply information about its parent organization, the International Youth Hostel Federation, which operates 5,000 hostels in 61 countries.

30. Pacing yourself may be the most important key to successful touring. Depending on mileage and terrain, divide the overall trip and each particular day into segments. Balance the long rides with the short, the hills with the flats.

31. Pacing also refers to riding style. Maintain good form and choose gears that permit a cadence of 75 to 90 rpm no matter what the terrain. Spinning a lower gear conserves energy and prevents muscle and joint injury when riding day after day.

32. If you long to take a bike tour but aren't sure you can afford its various expenses, here are some ideas for saving hundreds of dollars.

- Research your route so you can avoid pricey tourist traps.
- Anticipate unique problems and be prepared. For example, if you're allergic to bee stings, pack special medication and avoid emergency room expenses.
- Recruit several friends to accompany you and share all costs.
- To avoid an expensive parts failure, have your bike professionally inspected and serviced before you leave.
- Pack basic repair tools and know how to use them.

- If you'll be staying in motels, make advance reservations to get the cheapest rate.
- Pack a tent and stay in low-cost campgrounds, not fancy recreational vehicle parks.
- Check out small-town public facilities that may allow a free overnight stay, such as the grounds of parks, courthouses, fire stations, and schools.
- Compile the addresses of all your high school classmates, aunts, uncles, or cousins thrice removed. After you let them know you'll be pedaling near their homes, overnight invites are sure to follow.
- When stopping at a restaurant, always ask to see a menu before being seated so you're sure the prices are within your budget.
- Shop at roadside produce stands and farmers' markets for the most reasonably priced foods.
- Prepare your own meals using a pot, kitchen utensils, some charcoal, or a backpacking stove.

33. Perhaps the best source of free lodging is churches. Most have bathrooms, showers, and kitchens, and the hospitality is unequaled. In addition, congregational breakfasts and dinners are usually inexpensive and always filling.

34. When approaching someone for a favor, make sure they know you're a bicycle tourist. For some reason, most people are friendlier and less suspicious of cyclists.

35. A cheerful, outgoing personality will make you richer than any laundry list of money-saving tips. Strangers have been known to invite cyclists to family reunions, picnics, and into their homes. It takes just a little effort to bring out the generosity in people.

36. To gauge your current fitness and determine how much training you might need for the tour you're planning, determine its average daily mileage and ride this distance three times in one week.

37. Weekly training for touring should consist of two or three long rides (equal to the typical distance and pace you'll ride during your trip) for endurance, and one or two short, high-intensity workouts to improve strength and riding skills. These might include hard charges up hills, sprints, or time trials. One weekend day should be reserved for an extralong ride to accustom you to extended periods in the saddle.

38. Ride a fully loaded bike on one long training ride each week. This will build strength and familiarize you with the idiosyncrasies of handling the weight.

39. A 50-pound load doesn't allow you the luxury of standing and working the bike from side to side on hills, so during training get used to climbing while sitting and spinning your granny gear.

40. A 1-to-1 low gear ratio (e.g., 28-tooth chainring and 28-tooth rear cog) is necessary if your route has hills. Lower gearing—a larger rear cog and/or smaller inner chainring—is wise for mountainous terrain.

41. Consider a mountain bike for extended touring, thereby benefiting from its sturdiness and ability to handle a heavy load. The ideal model will have chainstays that are long enough to allow your heels to clear the rear panniers. Braze-on mounts for front and rear racks are a convenience, but their absence shouldn't eliminate a bike from consideration since clamp-on racks are available.

42. If you are sending your bike ahead, the best cardboard shipping box is the kind new bikes come in. These are usually available for no charge at bike shops. Avoid using the flimsy, unwieldy boxes the airlines sell.

43. You may be able to avoid excess baggage fees charged by airlines if your boxed bike weighs less than 60 pounds, the box is relatively small, and it is your only piece of check-in luggage. Hence, once your bike is inside the box, surround it with as many of your personal items as possible. Protect clothes from chain grease by putting them in plastic bags.

44. Of all the essentials for saving time and frustration on a trip across the country, the following are most important.

   • Good route: The two most popular cross-country

courses are the TransAmerica Bicycle Trail (4,250 miles) and the Northern Tier Bicycle Route (4,400 miles), both developed by Bikecentennial (Box 8308-AQ, Missoula, MT 59807). If you decide to plan your own route, choose county and secondary roads as much as possible.
- Adequate time and money: Loaded touring, where you carry camping and cooking gear, usually costs about $15 per day ($5 for campsites, $10 for food). Light touring, where indoor accommodations are used, generally costs about $45 per day. Budget an additional $5 per day for incidentals, and carry an emergency fund of at least $100 in traveler's checks.
- Physical preparedness: Start training at least one month before the trip is to begin, building up to day tours of 55 to 65 miles. Include at least one multiday dress rehearsal, riding your loaded bike on hilly terrain. Then start the trip with a few short, easy days. This provides the chance for necessary adjustments and helps you get into the rhythm of cross-country cycling.
- Proper equipment: Wheels and gearing are the most common sources of trouble on cross-country tours. Use wide, Kevlar-belted tires and wheels built of strong rims, 14-gauge spokes, and high-quality hubs. Choose an 18- or 21-speed drivetrain that will allow you to maintain a cadence of 75 to 90 rpm no matter what the terrain or wind conditions. The low gear should be in the 20- to 30-inch range.
- Proper attitude: You must be prepared to accept anything, because on the backroads of America you're liable to find it.

45. To prevent maps from taking up so much space in your panniers, trim away the unnecessary parts. Then throw away each map when you're done with it.

46. Contrary to popular belief, wind more often comes from the east than west in the country's heartland. On each coast, however, it more commonly blows west to east. Thus, on a cross-country trip, the direction you ride will determine whether you have tailwind assistance at the beginning and end of the ride, or in the middle.

47. There are two keys to keeping a useful, informative journal during a tour: Be honest and be consistent. Don't be self-conscious in what you write or you'll miss adding life to factual information. Make it a rule to spend at least 15 minutes each day recording what you've accomplished, seen, and felt.

48. If you don't like to write, keep a small tape recorder in your handlebar bag. Then you can record your ideas and feelings quickly and effortlessly.

49. A standard first-aid kit for tourists should contain a selection of adhesive bandages, several butterfly skin closures, a packet of sterile 4-inch-square gauze pads, a couple of Telfa pads, a roll of 3-inch gauze, a roll of 2-inch athletic tape, liquid soap, alcohol prep swabs, a small container of petroleum jelly, and a tube of antibiotic ointment. Also useful is a pair of paramedic or EMT scissors. Medications should include a laxative, antacid, something to fight diarrhea, an antihistamine, a painkiller such as aspirin or ibuprofen, and a snakebite kit.

50. Store personal medication and other small items in plastic vials (available from drugstores), and leakable supplies in zip-close plastic bags. Just to be safe, put everything into a larger zip-close bag and stow it in the same place every trip.

51. Touring alone, rather than with a group, has several important advantages. Solo, you can pedal easily without worrying that you are disrupting someone else's style or schedule. You start, rest, and finish when you want, and change plans and routes as often as you please.

52. When a thunderstorm approaches, immediately seek shelter in a car or substantial building. Once you hear thunder, the storm is within 15 miles, and it may be moving as fast as 50 mph.

53. Without a building or car to get into, take these precautions to reduce chances of being struck by lightning.

- Move to lower ground.

- Avoid metal objects such as wire fences, guardrails, and your bike.
- Avoid lone trees or isolated stands of tall ones.
- Take cover in a ravine or under small trees or shrubs.
- Don't huddle in a group.
- Squat on the balls of your feet, or kneel with your toes touching the ground. This minimizes the chance of the bolt passing through your heart.

54. Before choosing a map, decide how much detail you need. Some people can ride across the country using only state maps such as those found at gas stations, while others need more exact guides indicating traffic patterns, rural roads, and topography. In general, a cycling map should indicate essentials such as food stops and lodging. But to preserve your adventure you don't want so much detail that you know what's around every bend.

55. Use topographic maps to get an overall picture of the terrain. These maps have contour lines that connect points of the same elevation. When these lines are spaced far apart, it means the landscape is flat or rolling. When they're tightly bunched, it's hilly.

56. For a free index and order form for topographic maps, contact the U.S. Geological Survey, Distribution Branch, Box 25286, Federal Center, Building 41, Denver, CO 80225.

57. For road maps customized for cycling, contact Bikecentennial, Box 8308-AQ, Missoula, MT 59807.

21 CHECKPOINTS FOR SAFE COMMUTING AND CITY CYCLING

1. The first rule for safe commuting on roads with heavy traffic is to be sure drivers can see you. Wear bright colors such as red, yellow, and orange, and use lights and reflectors when light is low.

2. Ride defensively, but this doesn't mean timidly. Be predictable and go about your business with a self-assurance that shows you know what you're doing. This will help motorists feel comfortable sharing the road with you.

3. Ride far enough into the traffic lane to avoid being struck by opening doors on cars that are parallel parked. You'll likely attract some honks from following motorists who don't understand why you won't pull to the right to let them pass immediately, but at least you know they see you.

4. Don't gain ground at red lights by passing a line of cars on the right. It's illegal, and you can get "doored" from either side. It also irritates motorists, because they have to pass you again after the light changes.

5. When you stop for a light, move to the center of your lane. This prevents vehicles from edging forward, trapping you between them and the curb. When the light changes, accelerate to your cruising speed before moving right to allow them to pass.

6. Always ride in as straight a line as possible so motorists can sense how far left they have to go to get past you safely. Never weave in and out of cars that are intermittently parallel parked.

7. Earn motorists' respect for yourself and all cyclists by liberally using hand signals for turns, swerves, and braking maneuvers. Use your left arm (finger pointed) to signal left turns and braking (palm facing backward) and your right arm to signal right turns. Forget that business about signaling right turns with the left arm. It originated because motorists can't reach across to the right window.

8. Look through the rear windows of parked cars for someone who might throw open a door or to see a pedestrian about to step from between cars. Since most potential hazards appear to your front, learn to scrutinize each side street and driveway for cars, kids, and dogs.

9. When you see a car stopped at a cross street, watch its front wheels, where it's possible to spot even slight forward movement. If you see any, get ready to brake, swerve, and/or shout.

10. Forget horns, bells, and whistles as warning devices. They take too long to use and most aren't loud enough to be effective. A loud scream originating deep in your diaphragm is instant and requires no hands.

11. Resist making a profane gesture or obscene shout when a motorist harasses you. You may think you're doling out punishment, but psychologists say otherwise. It actually tells the hostile driver he or she succeeded and encourages more of the same action. Likewise, don't meekly pull off the road. Such a retreat proves that your ride has been ruined, and for the driver this is another form of reward.

12. The best course of action when you're harassed is to swallow your anger and continue riding as if nothing happened. As the hostile driver goes by, continue in a straight line, stay cool, and try to memorize the vehicle's license plate number. Chant it for the next 10 miles if necessary.

13. To clean up upon arriving at work or school (assuming a shower isn't available), use a deodorant soap and washcloth at the sink. Or, douse a washcloth with rubbing alcohol and wipe yourself down. This will cool your body while killing odor-causing germs.

14. A useful skill in traffic is the "instant turn." This evasive action comes in handy when a car passes you and immediately turns right, or when an oncoming car turns left across your path, leaving you no time to brake. Steer left briefly to create a lean angle, then immediately turn right with the car to avoid a collision. (See illustration 9-1.)

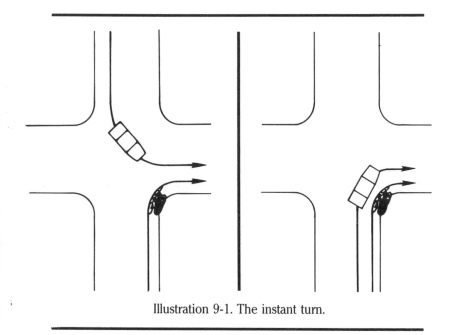

Illustration 9-1. The instant turn.

15. The only valid reason not to commute by bicycle is that you don't want to. To prove it, here are ten common excuses and their easy solutions.

Excuse: I can't afford a special commuter bike. *Solution:* Use your present bike, or buy a used "beater." It needn't cost much as long as it works reliably.

Excuse: I have to dress nice for work and can't stuff my good clothes in panniers. *Solution:* Drive to work one day each week, leave a week's worth of clean clothes, and take the dirty stuff home.

Excuse: There's no secure place to park my bike. *Solution:*

It may not seem so, but check for a storage closet or out-of-the-way corner somewhere. Or stash it with a friend who lives nearby, a bike shop, or at another business that accommodates cyclists.

Excuse: It's not safe to ride in rush-hour traffic. *Solution:* It's usually possible to get from home to work on less-congested back streets or secondary roads. You may have to ride a few extra miles, but they will bring more exercise and enjoyment.

Excuse: I like to sleep, and I'd have to get up earlier if I rode my bike. *Solution:* An extra few minutes of sleep aren't nearly as refreshing as a brisk morning ride. And your evening ride home will leave you relaxed, so you'll sleep more soundly. Quality over quantity.

Excuse: Due to my work schedule, I'd have to ride in the dark. *Solution:* Wear light-colored, reflective clothing, attach lights and reflectors, and use a route that's well lit by streetlights.

Excuse: I don't like riding in the cold/rain/snow. *Solution:* Don't commute by bike on nasty days. But you may start looking forward to your daily rides so much that you invest in a rainsuit, wind jacket, tights, mittens, balaclava, booties, thermal socks, goggles, and the like.

Excuse: My commute is too far to ride. *Solution:* Consider cycling only partway. Drive to within a reasonable distance, park, and ride the rest. Maybe you can even take a bus or train to where your bike is stashed.

Excuse: I live too close to work to make riding worthwhile. *Solution:* Take the longer, more scenic route.

Excuse: People will think I'm weird if I ride a bike to work. *Solution:* These days, your coworkers will probably admire you because you're doing something that's healthful, economical, and protective of the environment and natural resources.

16. Because most commuting takes place early or late in the day, sun glare can be a hazard, making it difficult for motorists to see you. Eliminate this risk by altering your route so you never ride directly into the sun.

17. Ride well into the lane when traffic is stop-and-go. A cyclist can usually move as fast as cars in such conditions, so don't hug the curb where you're less visible and drivers are tempted to squeeze by.

18. To enhance your safety on the road, beware of the three most common driver errors that threaten cyclists.

  - Turning left in front of an oncoming cyclist who's going straight through an intersection
  - Failing to obey a stop sign and pulling in front of a rider
  - Passing a cyclist and immediately turning right into his or her path

19. If you have the right of way at an intersection, don't coast through or drivers may assume they can cut in front of you. Keep pedaling, but be prepared to brake.

20. Use your ears as an early warning system. Tip-offs to danger include engines revving or slowing, squealing tires, and gear changes.

21. If you ever wondered how dangerous it is to cycle in a polluted urban area, take a deep breath and relax. A study found that riding a bike in New York City is far less damaging to the lungs than smoking cigarettes or even being in a room full of smokers. In fact, the amount of carbon monoxide in the blood of midtown bike messengers actually declined during the course of a day, prompting speculation that hard breathing may expel pollutants from the lungs.

88 TIPS TO KEEP YOUR HEALTH IN GEAR

1. Massage your legs. Pro racers usually receive a daily massage to promote muscle recovery. But when a masseur isn't available, they massage themselves. Former U.S. champion Thomas Prehn recommends sitting on a bed with your back against the wall. For each leg, massage the calf first, then move to the knee and thigh, always stroking toward the heart.

2. If your legs are shaved, use oil when you massage them. Thomas Prehn's favorite is warm sesame oil. Afterward, wipe it off with rubbing alcohol to prevent it from clogging your pores.

3. Stay limber by stretching. Two sessions a day are recommended, one when you get out of bed, the other after training. Each 10- to 15-minute session should stretch the legs, lower back, stomach, and arms. In addition to increasing on-bike comfort and efficiency, stretching can help prevent muscle and joint injuries.

4. To help prevent muscle soreness after a strenuous ride, pedal easily during the final 10 minutes and avoid hills.

5. In cold weather, if you're comfortable in the first mile, you're overdressed.

6. A cotton cycling cap can provide a lot of warmth. Much body heat is lost through the head. Carry it in your jersey pocket when you don't need it.

7. Apply a thin coat of petroleum jelly to exposed skin to keep it from becoming chapped.

8. When using multiple layers of clothing, wear polypropylene (not Lycra or cotton) against the skin for proper wicking of perspiration.

9. If you're going from sea level to high altitude (5,000 feet or more), expect your performance to suffer. The reason is not that there's less oxygen in the air; rather, the amount of atmospheric pressure forcing it into your lungs is decreased. Thus, your body receives less oxygen with each inhalation and must increase respiration and heart rate to compensate. The result can be pronounced breathing problems, fatigue, headaches, and even nausea.

10. To acclimate to high altitude before a race or other hard ride, it's best to undertake a special three-week conditioning program. The first week should be limited to slow rides, the second to harder ones, and the third to rest and recovery. This will allow your body gradually to become more efficient at utilizing the available oxygen.

11. To minimize other effects of high altitude, drink plenty of fluids to fend off dehydration, and wear light-colored clothing and helmet covers to shield your body from the sun.

12. Here are several good ways to clean a water bottle and help eliminate the plastic smell and taste.
    * Fill the bottle with hot water and put in four drops of bleach. Let it stand overnight, then rinse with alternating hot and cold water to break the molecular surface tension of any remaining bleach. This kills bacteria and leaves no taste.
    * If the idea of bleach doesn't appeal to you, let the bottle stand overnight with a teaspoon of lemon or lime juice in the water.
    * Rinse the bottle with warm water containing a teaspoon of baking soda. Then put it upside down in your bottle cage to dry.
    * Wash the bottle in a dishwasher every time you use it.

13. Each year there are approximately 90,000 car/bike accidents, according to the National Highway Traffic Safety

Administration. Here are eight ways to make sure you don't contribute to this statistic.

- Become a part of the traffic instead of just riding beside it. For instance, use the specially designated traffic lanes to make turns. Assert your right to move out of bike lanes whenever necessary.
- Wear brightly colored apparel.
- Slow down at intersections.
- Don't antagonize motorists with obscene shouts or gestures.
- Use hand signals well in advance.
- Make sure to use a good-quality light if you ride at night. Reflectors alone aren't sufficient.
- Avoid congested public roads and peak rush-hour traffic.
- Always wear a helmet.

14. If you get something in your eye and your natural reflexes (blinking and tears) don't dispel it, stop and wash it out with clean water from your bottle. If no water is available, pull your upper eyelid over your lower one, then roll your eye. This often deposits the object on the lower lid.

15. Need a mirror for any reason, such as relocating a wayward contact lens or finding a gnat in your eye? There's one on the driver's-side door of almost every parked car. You'll also find one in most gas stations, convenience stores, and the like.

16. Upon finishing a ride, brush your teeth before drinking and eating. This will cleanse your mouth of mucus, plus the dust, grit and other airborne stuff that you've been breathing.

17. To prevent numbness in the hands ("handlebar palsy" or ulnar neuropathy), which is caused by the compression and hyperextension of the nerves passing through the wrist into the palm, cushion the pressure points. Padded gloves and handlebar covers go a long way toward solving the problem. So does frequently changing your grip on the bar.

18. Use this checklist to solve genital numbness, which is

caused by pressure from the saddle on the two pudendal nerves in the crotch.

- Is the saddle too far from the handlebar? If you have to lean forward excessively to reach the bar, it causes the nose of the saddle to press on the nerves. Install a shorter stem, or move the saddle forward if it won't adversely affect your pedaling position.
- Is the nose of the saddle tipped up or down? If up, it is probably increasing pressure. If down, you are probably sliding forward onto the nerves. Set the saddle parallel to the top tube.
- Is the saddle too high? This will cause you to ride farther foward to get closer to the pedals, or rock side to side in order to reach them. Lower the saddle until you can pedal backward smoothly with your heels.
- Is the saddle wide enough for proper support? With a seat that's narrower than your pelvic structure you have no chance to be suppported correctly. You may have better success with one of the so-called anatomically designed saddles.
- Is the saddle properly padded? The best have a layer of gel or dense foam between a pliable plastic base and a flexible outer covering. Hard, weakly padded, inexpensive plastic saddles are no bargain when you consider the number of hours you ride your bike.
- Are you riding intelligently? During a long ride, periodically stand out of the saddle for a minute or so to relieve pressure. Something so simple works amazingly well.

19. At the first sign of foot discomfort on a long ride, slightly loosen your shoelaces or straps and, if you have them, toe straps. Feet tend to swell as the miles go by, and it's the resulting tightness and restricted blood flow that cause pain and the sensation of heat.

20. If you have back pain when you ride in the drops for more than a few minutes, raise the stem until its top is just an inch or two below the top of the saddle.

21. If your triceps muscles become sore, it may mean your stem is too long. Conversely, if it's too short, your shoulder muscles will bother you.

22. To prevent a sore neck, don't keep your head in a fixed, straight-ahead position. Cock it slightly to one side for a couple of minutes, then to the other. You'll find it takes less effort to hold your head this way, especially when you're riding in the drops.

23. Wear sunglasses to feel fresher on long rides. Squinting into the sun and wind taxes the optical and facial muscles, contributing significantly to fatigue.

24. When you need to take a pain reliever, decide whether swelling also needs to be treated. If so, try aspirin, ibuprofen, or an anti-inflammatory prescription drug. Acetaminophen (Tylenol) will reduce pain but not swelling.

25. If you drink alcohol, limit yourself to no more than two beverages per day, the equivalent of 24 ounces of beer, 12 ounces of wine, or 2 ounces of whiskey. Research shows that one healthful effect of regular exercise, namely lower blood pressure, is nullified for those who drink larger quantities.

26. Saddle soreness results from slight bruising and is something all new or infrequent cyclists experience, but it'll pass as riding becomes more regular. Saddle sores, however, can happen to any rider who neglects to use proper equipment and hygiene, so follow these tips.

- Dress right. Wear shorts with a natural or synthetic chamois liner, and do not wear underwear while riding.
- Keep clean. Wash your crotch and the shorts before every ride. Have two pairs of shorts so one is always clean and ready.
- Dry your shorts inside out in the sun. Ultraviolet radiation kills bacteria. (If your shorts are Lycra, hang them inside to dry, since the sun can damage this particular fabric.)
- Avoid wearing tight pants when not riding. Loose clothing permits air circulation and helps keep you dry, thus inhibiting the growth of bacteria. Sleeping without underwear may also be helpful.
- Inspect your bike. If your saddle is too low or high, angled up or down, or too distant from the handlebar,

this can cause excess movement and the chafing that leads to sores.

- Ride smart. Stand up when cycling over railroad tracks and rough patches, and make it a habit to pedal out of the saddle for 30 seconds at least once every half hour.
- Use a good-quality saddle. This means firm enough to keep your body stable, yet flexible enough to absorb your weight. It should be wide enough in back for good support, but narrow in front where your legs need room. Overly wide, cushy seats can cause rocking and chafing.

27. If you get a saddle sore, wash the area a couple of times a day with an antibacterial soap such as Hibiclens or Betadine Surgical Scrub. Keep your crotch as dry as possible between cleanings. Don't cover the sore with salves or ointments because these may actually keep bacteria alive.

28. Don't apply alcohol to saddle sores or your crotch in general. It can dry the skin too much and cause additional irritation that can lead to more sores.

29. If a saddle sore doesn't respond quickly to treatment, take a couple of days off the bike.

30. On a cool and windy day, pick a route that takes you into the wind during the first half and with it the second. The opposite will mean you face the wind after becoming hot and sweaty, which can result in hypothermia even when the temperature is in the 60s.

31. If you're under 18 and suffer from leg muscle cramps when cycling, you may be pushing too hard for your age. Since muscles don't mature until about 18, reduce the duration and intensity of rides just enough to eliminate cramping.

32. If you're suffering from Achilles tendon pain, try raising the saddle. This may seem to defy logic, but here's the thinking: With a lower saddle, you ride with a more horizontal foot position, and this puts more strain on the tendon. The foot is at a right angle, which creates more stretch and force on the calf muscle and tendon. Raising the saddle keeps the foot pointed slighty downward so your calf is no longer in a stretched position, thus decreasing the force and releasing some of the tension.

33. Don't take salt tablets. Even in sweating off 2 pounds, you lose only 1 gram of sodium, or the equivalent of half a teaspoon of salt. What's more, because of decreased blood volume and the conservation of sodium by the kidneys, sodium concentration in the blood actually increases during exercise. Salt tablets can dangerously raise your sodium level.

34. If you suffer from chondromalacia (a degeneration of the cartilage under the kneecap), cycling should help, not hurt, as long as you (1) adjust the saddle so your knee remains only slightly bent at the bottom of the pedal stroke, and (2) avoid big gears and long, steady climbs whenever possible. The key is to spin in moderate gears.

35. Stretching is beneficial for cyclists, but if you're planning a short ride you don't have to go through a 20-minute routine. Beforehand, try a sustained quadriceps stretch and hold it for at least 20 seconds. Do the same for each calf and ankle, and one for the shoulders and neck. Then do a couple more stretches after you ride.

36. Consistency is the key when it comes to getting benefits from stretching. You're better off stretching a few minutes every day than going through a big 30-minute routine once every three days.

37. Proper stretching technique is to go to the point where you feel the stretch, then back off slightly. Everything should be relaxed. If you stretch to the point of pain, your body thinks it's going to be injured, so it tries to contract against the force. You end up with the opposite response to what you want.

38. Make sunscreen a part of your summer cycling kit. Most brands are rated numerically between 1 and 15 (the higher the number, the greater the protection against burning ultraviolet rays). Apply it to your arms, legs, hands, face, and especially the back of your neck.

39. During a tour, when the forecasted high temperature (in Fahrenheit) and humidity total 160 or more (for example, 90°F plus 90 percent humidity equals 180), it may be wise to amend the day's ride to avoid heat-related maladies.

Under such conditions, you should usually start cycling earlier in the morning, rest during the hottest part of the day, and complete the ride in the evening.

40. To improve your performance, especially on hills, lose weight. The ideal amount of body fat for an elite male rider is 6 to 9 percent and for a woman, 11 to 14 percent. In contrast, the average sedentary adult male has 20 percent fat while his female counterpart has 25 percent.

41. Percentage of body fat can't be determined with a bathroom scale. You need to have it calculated by a professional using one of three common methods: underwater weighing, skin-fold measurement, or electrical impedence. To have yourself measured, check local hospitals, athletic clubs, college physiology departments, and sportsmedicine physicians.

42. A good way to accurately determine your individual fluid needs is to weigh yourself before and after a hot-weather, long-distance ride. Remember that a pint of water equals a pound. If you've lost more than a pound or two on a hot day, increase your fluid intake proportionately.

43. The patella tendon, which attaches the kneecap to your shinbone, is crucial for pedaling because the entire force of the quadriceps contraction is dependent on its strength. This is why the tendon is occasionally injured. Therapy includes ice massage, anti-inflammatory medication, and benign quadriceps exercises such as straight leg raises in multiple directions. To recover fully you need to abstain from squatting, kneeling, going up and down stairs, and exercising on knee extension machines. When cycling, raise your saddle slightly and spin against a low resistance.

44. Dressing in layers is the secret for taking the danger out of temperatures as low as 10 below zero. Start with long underwear made from a material such as polypropylene or Thermax that wicks perspiration away from the skin. Then add insulating layers of wool or synthetic and cover it all with a breathable windbreaker. Don't overdress. As a rule, you should feel slightly chilly during the initial mile.

45. You dehydrate surprisingly fast in cold weather, and water freezes quickly. To keep it liquid, put your bottle inside an insulated camera lens case, and carry an additional water bottle in a pocket between your inner and outer layers of clothing.

46. If you tend to get an earache when riding in cool or windy weather, filling your ears with cotton is the best way to prevent it. Also, don't clean the wax from your ears with swabs or drops. This will leave them vulnerable to cold air and wind.

47. If you donate blood, expect a 5 to 10 percent decrease in your exercise capability for about two weeks. This will show up most in extended efforts such as time trials. If you donate blood frequently, beware of developing an iron deficiency. Have your doctor do a serum ferritin test to determine your iron level. If it's low, start taking an iron supplement or donate less often.

48. Sunscreens are necessary, but they interfere with perspiration. To reduce the amount of sunscreen you need, hang a handkerchief from the back of your helmet to cover your neck, and wear wraparound sunglasses. On skin areas that can't be covered, apply a waterproof sunscreen with the highest sun protection factor (SPF). Just a little will give maximum protection. To allow perspiration, use less on the inside of arms and legs.

49. To reduce the chance of saddle sores, minimize sweating and chafing. The former can be controlled by applying powder to your skin, or by riding in shorts with a polypropylene liner, which wicks moisture. The latter requires good-quality cycling shorts that are never worn twice before washing. Treating a natural chamois with petroleum jelly, lanolin, or a special "fat" made for the purpose will prolong its life and reduce abrasion.

50. To minimize danger from carbon monoxide in the air, try to avoid roads with lots of traffic. Also realize that this type of pollution is greater in winter for three reasons: cold engines produce higher concentrations of the gas; other fuels are being used for heat; winds are lighter.

51. To reduce the breathing problems and eye irritation associated with high ozone levels, ride before the morning rush hour.

52.   If cycling seems to cause a runny nose similar to having a cold or allergy, you're probably suffering from vasomotor rhinitis. It is believed to be caused by an imbalance of nerve impulses to the nose. This results in overactive parasympathetic nerves, which are responsible for nasal secretion. Relief usually comes with a prescription drug known as ipatropium or Atrovent.

53.   Don't use motor oil to soften a new leather saddle. It contains a variety of additives designed to reduce engine wear, and some are toxic and should not be applied to the skin. Instead, use a white mineral oil that's free of potentially harmful additives.

54.   Don't drink from another person's water bottle. This practice can spread enteroviral infections, which are carried by fluids and have caused outbreaks of diseases such as aseptic meningitis.

55.   If you have varicose veins, it's possible that cycling could worsen the condition unless you take precautions. This is because of the buildup of venous pressure caused by pedaling and the bent-over position of the upper body (which can impede blood flow from the legs to the heart). To protect yourself, rest with your legs elevated above heart level after riding and at the end of the day. Walking after a ride is also helpful.

56.   Wear your sunglasses even on cloudy days. In fact, your eyes are more at risk from ultraviolet sun rays when it's overcast because they lose the natural protection that stems from squinting and blinking.

57.   On long rides, you must replace electrolytes. These are minerals (sodium, chloride, potassium) that carry an electrical charge that's necessary for muscle contraction and the maintenance of fluid levels. If you don't use a sports drink (or don't eat) on a long ride, you can suffer dangerous electrolyte imbalances such as a low blood sodium condition called hyponatremia. This results in lethargy, confusion, and muscle weakness.

58. There are several good reasons serious male cyclists traditionally shave their legs. One is to provide a smooth working surface for massage. Another is ease of treating road rash—if legs are already shaved, hair won't have to be removed before bandaging, and the stuff won't be entangled in the wound, which reduces the risk of infection. Some evidence even suggests that smooth skin slides better on pavement, thus reducing the severity of road rash. Hairless skin is also more aerodynamic and, let's admit it, revealing of leg muscles.

59. For first-time leg shavers, don't wait until the eve of a big event. The strange feel of the bedsheets will make it difficult to sleep. Use barbers' shears or clippers for the initial denuding, then razors and shaving cream to attack the stubble. A weekly once-over in the shower will keep you slick for the rest of the season.

60. "Road rash" isn't a rash at all. It's a common cycling abrasion in which outer layers of skin are scraped away as a result of sliding over a rough, gritty surface. This exposes deeper layers and damages blood vessels, which ooze and create the familiar red badge. Follow these steps to treat it.

A. First, thoroughly clean and disinfect the wound. This is much less painful if done within 30 minutes of the crash, since nerve endings will be numb from the trauma.

B. To prevent infection and scarring, scrub the wound hard with a rough washcloth or a medium/soft bristle brush. Apply a liberal amount of an antibacterial surgical soap such as Hibiclens or Betadine.

C. Next, apply an antibacterial ointment such as Neosporin. All these products are available without prescription.

D. Cover the cleaned abrasion with a nonstick sterile dressing such as Telfa or Second Skin. To prevent the wound from leaking onto clothes or bedsheets, cover the dressing with a layer of absorbent gauze for the first few days.

E. Change the dressing each morning and night. Apply more antibacterial ointment before covering the wound and check for signs of infection: tenderness, swollen red skin, a sensation of heat. If you detect any of these, consult a doctor.

F. To minimize scarring, keep the area moist and don't let

a scab form. As new skin starts to form, apply Saratoga ointment and a light gauze. This zinc-oxide-based salve will prevent a scab. Then use a moisturizer on new skin for a week.

61. For upper-body protection against road rash, wear a light, cotton T-shirt under your cycling jersey. This usually lessens abrasion in a fall because it allows the outer garment to slide against the inner one instead of your skin.

62. Make sure your tetanus vaccination is current. If you should crash and suffer cuts or road rash and it's been several years since your last tetanus shot, get one within 24 hours of the accident. Tetanus bacteria produce powerful toxins that can do great harm.

63. The hazards of consuming alcohol are well known, and here's another one: It can hurt your cycling performance by disturbing your body's delicate balance of iron and other vital elements. It also causes you to lose a great deal of water, which can result in dehydration. In fact, your body needs 8 ounces of water to metabolize 1 ounce of alcohol.

64. If you party hard on Friday night, don't expect to ride well again until Sunday. Studies show that it takes at least 36 hours before the performance-impairing effects of alcohol wear off.

65. A lack of sleep won't necessarily hurt your cycling. Researchers have found that strength, reaction time, aerobic ability, and heart rate don't change significantly even after 60 hours of sleep deprivation. What does change is mood and perception. On long rides, this may inhibit performance.

66. According to some researchers, women athletes perform best 12 to 15 days after their menstrual flow has ended. A woman who rides during her period increases the odds for sub-par performance.

67. Stay off the bike during the two or three (on average) colds you'll catch each year. But if you must ride, take it easy because viruses often travel to muscles, where they cause microscopic damage and fatigue. In fact, one study showed a 15 percent strength loss among people who recently had a virus.

68. For losing weight, select the gear in which you can generate the fastest speed for the time you're riding. Contrary to the popular theory that low-intensity exercise causes the body to rely primarily on fat for energy, don't restrict your intensity in an attempt to burn a higher percentage of stored fat. It's total caloric consumption that's most important, and it will increase with your effort.

69. If your cleats and saddle are properly adjusted, knee noises aren't anything to worry about unless they're accompanied by pain.

70. If you suffer from lower-back pain caused by riding, you may have a strength imbalance between your stomach muscles and those that lift your legs. The best cure is a daily dose of "crunch" sit-ups. Lie on the floor and simply bend your knees 90 degrees. Roll your shoulders off the floor, and stop before the small of your back leaves the ground.

71. An occasional bout of dizziness, especially when you stand up, is usually nothing to be alarmed about. It's probably vasovagal syncope, a condition that occurs when your blood pressure is temporarily too low to get enough blood to your brain. It's common in people with slow pulse rates and low blood pressure. In other words, fit cyclists. If you feel it happening, lie down or sit with your head down until the dizziness passes.

72. Keep riding to improve your cholesterol and thereby lower your risk of heart disease. A year-long study found that subjects who cycled 1 hour a day, four or five times a week, experienced a 13 percent increase in their HDL, or so-called "good" cholesterol that polices your system and removes the harmful LDL type. This translates to a 10 to 20 percent reduction in heart disease risk.

73. If your saddle height seems correct for only one leg, you may have a significant leg-length discrepancy. For a quick check, remove your shoes and socks, lie on your back, then have a friend pick up your legs by the heels and shake them gently. When they're laid down together, your friend will be able to judge if one leg seems longer.

74. It's not uncommon to have a leg-length discrepancy of ¼ inch or more. This can cause your body to make some anatomical adjustments, which could result in injury to muscles or cartilage, particularly in the lower back. To measure your discrepancy, lie on your back and have a helper run a finger along the ridge of your pelvis starting at your side and moving toward the front of your body. Just as the crest begins to dive toward your feet, there is a sharp, bony projection. Measure from this point to the bottom of the prominent bone on the outside of your ankle. Repeat the procedure three times. If any two measurements are the same, discard the odd one. Otherwise, average all three. Repeat for the other leg and compare the figures.

75. Ignore a leg-length discrepancy of ⅛ inch or less. If it's ⅛ to ⅜ inch, you should correct 75 to 100 percent of the difference even if you have no problems or symptoms. If the difference is more than ⅜ inch, or if you're concerned about any unexplained pains you think might be related to a discrepancy, seek help from a podiatrist.

76. To correct a leg-length discrepancy, make height adjustments at the ball of the foot, not the heel, because this is where you contact the pedal. A discrepancy of ⅛ inch can be corrected by using a thicker or double insole in the shoe of your shorter leg. Correct differences of ⅜ inch or so by sliding the cleat of your longer leg rearward about ⅜ inch. For larger discrepancies, raise your shorter leg by placing a rubber or plastic block between the cleat and shoe. It's best to combine the different remedies so the problem will be corrected without radically modifying pedal position or the fit of your shoes.

77. Take precautions to avoid catching a cold, which can set back your training by a week or more. Most colds aren't spread by coughing or sneezing but by hand contact. Thus, during cold season, it's a good idea to wash your hands several times daily and avoid touching your mouth, eyes, and nose until after you do.

78. Got sore knees? The sound your joints make may provide a clue to the problem. A popping sound indicates osteoarthritis, while a noise like Velcro pulling apart suggests rheumatoid arthritis. A healthy knee sounds like a well-oiled seesaw.

79. If you experience pain along the outside of your knee, it's likely to be iliotibial band friction syndrome. This condition arises when the fibrous band along the outside of your upper leg rubs against the bony protrusion of the outside of the knee. It can result from improper cleat position, low seat height, bowed legs, wide hips, or a change in riding position. In some cases it's just a matter of doing too much riding too soon. The remedy is to apply ice, massage the area, take anti-inflammatory medication such as aspirin or ibuprofen, and correct your riding position. Also, some time off the bike may be in order. If ignored, the condition could become severe enough to require surgery.

80. To prevent neck discomfort while riding, never keep your head in the same position for a long time. Periodically tilt it to stretch and relax the muscles. Every so often on a straight, clear stretch of road, let your head drop to your chest—rotating it in one direction, then the other.

81. Inhaling frigid air during winter rides will not damage your throat and lungs. Exercise markedly increases body temperature, and the extra heat you generate instantly warms each breath you take.

82. Try to avoid riding on busy streets that are lined with trees. A university study found that overhanging limbs can trap dangerous levels of carbon monoxide.

83. As you age, staying fit will improve the quality of your life. Research has determined that older adults who exercise regularly have sharper minds than those who don't. The active group scored higher in tests for reasoning, memory, vocabulary, and reaction time.

84. Don't use bottled water in your bike bottles. It may seem like a healthy choice, but some brands contain organisms that multiply as the water temperature rises. These can trash your digestive system. Instead, use tap water. It's been purified to kill the offending organisms.

85. Men needn't worry that cycling can somehow result in prostate cancer. There's no known connection. Some doctors have speculated that cycling may aggravate prostatitis (an inflammation of the prostate gland, located at the base of the urethra), but again there's no proof.

86. If you have high blood pressure, think twice about riding after you've consumed caffeine. One study found that the caffeine equivalent of two cups of coffee, when combined with exercise, resulted in blood pressure readings twice as high as those produced by exercise alone.

87. Relieve your feet by occasionally not pushing down for several strokes. By only pulling up, pressure is reduced on your soles and blood circulation is enhanced.

88. If you suffer from exercise-induced nausea, here are the probable causes and solutions.

- Slow gastric emptying. When you ride with a lot of food or fluid in your belly, the stomach and working muscles battle for extra blood. The muscles always win, so food sits and makes you feel sick. There will be less risk if you never ride hard after eating and you gradually condition your system to handle food during cycling.
- Aggravated stomach lining. When liquid sloshes in your stomach, its mucous membrane can become irritated. Solution: Don't drink on rough roads or trails.
- Lowered pH. Vigorous riding exhausts the fuel in cells and produces acids. If the level of exercise is so high that your body is unable to buffer these acids, your pH level will fall, triggering nausea, headache, restlessness, and weakness. Solution: Back off at the first sign of distress.
- Dehydration. If you're riding in hot weather and don't drink enough, you'll become nauseated. And once your stomach is upset, you won't want to put anything in it, so the problem is compounded. Solution: Drink early and often on every ride.
- Anxiety. Preevent butterflies can stress your system just as much as high-intensity exercise and heat. Solution: If you tend to get this nervous, eat only easily digestible foods and do it about 3 hours before the start.

64 TIPS
ON WHAT TO EAT
AND WHEN

1. If you're interested in losing a few pounds, schedule your rides for midday. Not only will you burn calories, but the exercise will suppress your appetite. Afterward, you'll be surprisingly satisfied with lunch consisting of an apple or a cup of low-calorie yogurt.

2. The most nutritious fast foods are Chinese, Mexican, and Italian. These generally have less fat and are higher in energy-yielding carbohydrate than other cuisines.

3. When mixing sports drinks, put a less concentrated solution into the bottle(s) you'll drink last. Drinks always taste sweeter the longer you ride, and what seems pleasant initially can taste syrupy three hours later.

4. To save calories, substitute plain low-fat yogurt for sour cream and mayonnaise. Also, try spreading yogurt on your toast instead of butter or jam.

5. When the temperature makes full-finger gloves necessary, unwrap, slice, and repackage your snacks before riding. This makes it easier to grab a bite-size morsel while cycling.

6. To satisfy a cookie craving, eat fig bars or graham crackers, which are relatively low in fat.

7. Test specific sports drinks or energy foods long before an important event because some kinds might upset your stomach.

8. Freeze a bottle of water for hot rides. It'll slowly thaw and supply you with cool, refreshing liquid. Conversely, fill your bottle with hot water for cold rides.

9. Make your own carbohydrate drink with equal parts fruit juice and water. Apple and grape juices are popular; citrus juices tend to be harsh on an active stomach.

10. For optimum cooling and hydration, drink before as well as during rides. Consume about 16 ounces of water 1 to 2 hours before departing, and another 10 to 16 ounces with about 20 minutes to go.

11. Nibble solid food almost continuously during long rides, because if you start feeling hungry, it's too late to eat. Veteran racer Ian Jackson's favorite high-carbohydrate, easily digested on-bike foods include apples, fruit-filled pastries, and bananas. Former pro champion Thomas Prehn likes individually wrapped cream-filled oatmeal cookies. "They're perfect for riding, and they've got quite a lot of sugar, which I think is good during long rides," he says.

12. To lose 1 pound of body fat per week, burn approximately 3,500 more calories than you eat. Use table 11-1 to estimate how many calories you burn during your average workout.

TABLE 11-1.

Speed (mph)	Calories/minute	Calories/mile
22.5	24.0	64.0
21.0	19.5	55.7
18.5	15.0	48.6
16.0	19.5	39.3
12.0	6.0	30.0
8.3	3.75	27.0
6.0	2.65	26.5

13. Caffeine can help you tap the energy contained in stored fat, thus sparing precious carbohydrate that's stored in the form of glycogen. However, caffeine is a drug that some people don't tolerate well, so be careful if you don't normally drink coffee or other caffeinated beverages. Among its drawbacks, caffeine is a diuretic that can increase the chance of dehydration when you perspire.

14. On a very long ride, eat your food in this order: (1) sandwiches that contain meat or high-fat items such as peanut butter or cream cheese; (2) complex carbohydrates such as fruit, cookies, jam sandwiches, and energy bars; (3) simple sugars in the form of dextrose, glucose, or fructose wafers. This sequence is advocated by former U.S. national team coach Eddie Borysewicz, who says it gives you time-released fuel. As the first foods are being digested to supply food energy for the end of the ride, the faster-digesting second and third foods will go to work. In fact, he recommends nibbling a steady supply of sugar wafers right from the start to keep blood glucose levels high.

15. Never experiment with food or eating patterns on an important ride. Do it during training to find out what works . . . and what doesn't.

16. Don't wait to be thirsty before you drink. Drink much more often than you feel you need to; if you become thirsty during a ride you've made a big mistake. In hot weather you should be downing the better part of two water bottles per hour. Why so much? Dehydration is one of the primary—but most easily avoided—contributors to fatigue.

17. Diet in winter, not summer. Don't try to cut calories when you're riding nearly every day and doing long distance on weekends. You'll lose strength and ambition as surely as you lose weight.

18. Practice eating while on training rides, but keep in mind that choking is a danger for the inexperienced. It helps to clear the nasal passages just before eating because you have to breathe through your nose while chewing. Take small bites and chew well before you try to swallow.

19. Make it easier to eat while riding by carefully choosing and preparing your food. Slice your apples into bite-size pieces. Peel and divide your orange segments. Dried apricots are just the right size. Fruit-filled cookies are handy, too. Put these items into individual plastic sandwich bags.

20. When riding one-handed because you are reaching for food or water, grip the handlebar top next to the stem. This helps you sit up, and your movements won't be as likely to make the bike swerve and veer.

21. If you're riding in a paceline, wait until you're at the end of the line to do your drinking and reaching for food. You'll pose less danger to the other riders should you not hold a straight line.

22. Before a race or other strenuous ride, follow these rules.
   ● Eat enough to keep from feeling hungry before the start and during the first hour.
   ● Eat your meal two to three hours before the event. Emphasize moderate amounts of easily digested, complex carbohydrates (grains, fruit, potatoes, pasta, bread) so your upper intestinal tract is empty by event time. This helps prevent cramping and competition between muscles and the digestive system for a blood supply.
   ● Drink plenty of fluids with the meal, primarily water or fruit juice.

23. For a preride breakfast, try these racer favorites: rice pudding (212 calories per serving), yogurt (114 per cup), muffins (103 each), whole wheat toast (59 per slice), oatmeal (145 per cup), and whole-grain cereal (111 per serving).

24. Don't attempt to build an energy-rich carbohydrate reserve by eating large quantities at the preevent meal or during the event. It takes 12 to 24 hours to digest and store carbohydrate in the muscles and liver in the form of glycogen. In other words, your fuel tank is filled by the spaghetti, rice, potatoes, and bread that you eat during the two or three days leading up to the event.

25. Don't eat solid food for about 30 minutes before a substantial climb. It won't digest fast enough to give you energy, and your stomach may become upset when the going gets strenuous.

26. For short workouts it's probably better not to eat before-hand. Otherwise, some of your blood will be used for digestion rather than supplying oxygen and nutrients to your working muscles. Your legs don't need to be fed—they have enough stored glycogen (muscle fuel) for an hour-long ride.

27. Remember this rule of endurance cycling: You can ride 2½ hours without eating. But if you do eat, you can ride all day.

28. Your body's balance of electrolytes (the minerals, sodium, potassium, and chloride) is important because a disruption can result in decreased performance, cramps, and heat stroke, especially in hot-weather rides of 2 hours or more. Fortunately, electrolytes can easily be replaced by swigging a commercial electrolyte drink or eating fruits, vegetables, and their juices.

29. To estimate the number of calories burned while cycling, use this formula: A 150-pound adult riding at 15 mph burns 12 calories per minute. For each 15 pounds above 150, add 1.2 calories per minute. For each 15 pounds under 150, subtract 1.2 calories per minute.

30. You needn't be too choosy when selecting a sports drink. The type of simple sugar used in them doesn't seem to matter and is probably outweighed by other factors, such as flavor. If you like the taste, you're likely to drink more.

31. As you become fitter, your caloric needs are reduced, thus increasing your chance of packing on pounds if activity level decreases. For this reason, try these tips in winter to keep your weight under control.

- Eat less, but more often. Getting most of your daily calories from a single meal overloads your system and causes weight gain.
- Monitor your weight. If it increases each winter and decreases every spring, the extra poundage will gradually become easier to regain and harder to shed.
- Avoid "heavy" foods. These include sauces, dressings, and all fats—fare that's most popular during the winter holidays.
- Drink less alcohol. It's second to fat as a calorie source.

- Keep riding. Less saddle time is the most obvious reason for winter weight gain. If necessary, use an indoor trainer.
- Try other sports. An ideal alternative is swimming, because it burns four times as many calories per mile as running and there's minimal risk of injury.
- Don't eat as much. It's as simple as that. Continue to follow your high-carbohydrate diet, but reduce the quantity.

32.   Since you'll burn 3,000 to 5,000 calories per day on an extended tour, it's a rare chance to eat as much as you want. Of course, this isn't a license to pedal from one fast-food joint to the next. Instead, on tour aim for a diet of 65 percent carbohydrate, 25 percent protein, and 10 percent fat.

33.   Avoid drinking tea or coffee with meals. The tannic acid they contain inhibits the rate of absorption of iron by 50 percent. A low iron level is one of the most common deficiencies in the American diet. And since iron helps transport oxygen to muscles and tissues, a deficiency can impair cycling performance.

34.   Eat pasta before a big event and you'll be in the company of 83 percent of world-class cyclists, according to one poll. Their pasta of choice is spaghetti, and 60 percent of them eat it at least three times a week. Some favorites of the pros: pasta topped with honey, cold spaghetti with cottage cheese and cinnamon sugar, and pasta smothered with peanut butter.

35.   If you find yourself falling prey to binge eating, it can be a sign of overtraining. When you're training too much, your muscle tissue may break down faster than your body can replace it. This can cause an imbalance in the level of tryptophan, an amino acid that influences brain serotonin levels. Serotonin in turn regulates mood, pain sensitivity, and sleep. A lack of it may also lead to carbohydrate cravings. Thus, once some endurance athletes start eating, they find it difficult to stop.

36.   Eat five small meals each day rather than two or three large ones. Small meals spread calories throughout the day, providing a continuous source of energy. Processing a large meal can sap energy. Also, when you overload your digestive system, your body can only handle some of the calories. The rest are diverted into fat stores, which are less effective for fueling exercise.

37. At least 60 percent of your total daily calories should be in the form of carbohydrate, and it's best to choose the complex type rather than refined. The former includes fruits, vegetables, whole-grain breads and cereals, rice, pasta, and beans. Refined carbohydrate refers to sugar and sweets, such as candy, cake, and soda. During the first 24 hours after exhaustive exercise, there's no difference in glycogen (muscle fuel) synthesis between the two types. But after a day, complex carbohydrate promotes a significantly greater amount. In addition, it provides fiber and nutrients with the calories.

38. If you ride 1 hour a day, 60 percent of your daily calories should come from carbohydrate. If you ride 2 or more hours per day, up it to 70 percent.

39. If you're trying to lose weight, don't eat before a short- to medium-length ride. Researchers have found that when you eat before exercise, your body relies more on carbohydrate for energy. Thus, you burn less fat.

40. For those interested in weight loss, here's a list of ways to make sure you burn the maximum number of calories on a ride.

- Head for the hills. Climbing at any speed consumes more calories than cycling on flat ground at the same rate. Descents (especially if you pedal down) don't cancel this extra expenditure.
- Ride when it's windy. On a loop course, the energy saved with a tailwind doesn't quite match the extra calories burned against a headwind.
- Sit up. At speeds greater than 15 mph, an upright riding position results in significantly more calories burned than one low in the drops.
- Leave on your panniers. Anything that adds weight or wind resistance makes you use more energy.

- Don't draft. Riding in the slipstream of another rider reduces your workload by about 1 percent for each mile per hour.

41. Here are eight tips to help you modify your eating habits in a way that will not only eliminate excess body fat but also supply the energy to ride even better.

- Keep a food diary along with your training diary. Look for eating habits that disrupt good nutrition and an even caloric distribution throughout the day.
- Be realistic about the rate of weight loss. One pound per week is plenty.
- Replace bad foods with good ones. Decrease intake of calorically dense fat while increasing the amount of carbohydrate.
- Don't skip meals. In fact, eat three to five small ones daily.
- Decrease high-calorie portions. Have some pizza, ice cream, or cookies, but in moderation.
- Don't avoid the foods you crave. Reward yourself by eating them in moderation on special occasions, such as after your hardest ride of the week.
- Don't starve yourself. If you overeat one day, don't fast the next to compensate. Simply accept the transgression and start anew the morning after.
- Ride more. It's a way to lose weight if you find it too tough to significantly decrease your calorie consumption.

42. On a long ride, don't succumb to cravings for high-fat foods such as chips, cakes, nuts, meats, and cheeses. They're less efficient as fuel and take longer to digest, thus creating competition between your stomach and muscles for valuable, oxygen-rich blood. In the end, your muscles will win, but your stomach won't take the loss well. Nausea and vomiting may result.

43. To prevent the "bonk" (hypoglycemia), which is marked by tiredness, irritability, dizziness, nausea, confusion, and sometimes fainting, don't allow your blood glucose to become depleted. This is the substance that fuels the central nervous system. To keep your stores supplied, eat the same carbohydrate-rich foods used to produce glycogen, the fuel your muscles use.

44. To remedy the bonk, immediately eat or drink something rich in carbohydrate—bananas, fig bars, and fruit juice are good.

45. When you "hit the wall," you're essentially done for the day. Unlike the bonk, which is a depletion of readily renewed liver glycogen, hitting the wall results from exhaustion of muscle glycogen. This can be delayed by ingesting carbohydrate, but once it happens, it can only be remedied with rest and food.

46. In most cases there's no need to consume water if you're already using a sports drink. Studies show that while sports drinks do empty from the stomach slower than water, they're processed by the intestines faster. Thus, they're delivered to the bloodstream as quickly as water.

47. On rides lasting less than 2 hours, water is all you need because your existing fuel stores contain ample energy. But on longer rides, these stores will become depleted. When this happens, you need efficient fuel in a hurry. And this is what a sports drink gives you.

48. Tired of pasta? Here are two non-Italian cuisines that supply ample amounts of energy-producing carbohydrate.
- Asian. The major ingredients in Chinese food (rice, noodles, and vegetables) are rich in carbo. Small amounts of meat and fish are also used. This combination offers the necessary proportion of carbohydrate to protein and fat. Foods from Thailand, Korea, Vietnam, and India feature beans, rice, grains, vegetables, and breads, all of which are high in carbohydrate.
- Mexican. Tortillas, enchiladas, and chili (non-carne) are all top carbo dishes. Just be sure to avoid fried or refried dishes (they contain more fat) and those that have lots of meat or cheese.

49. The correct way to increase your consumption of energy-yielding foods ("carbohydrate load") for a major long-distance event is to begin six days before with a hard ride for about 90 minutes. On this day your food intake should be about 50 percent carbohydrate. Continue this diet for two days, but decrease your training to about 40 minutes per day to preserve your stores of glycogen (muscle fuel derived from carbohydrate). The next two days, reduce your training to about 20 minutes per day and consume 70 percent carbohydrate. To achieve this percentage, eat no more calories than normal but increase your intake of bread, fruit, vegetables, and other high-carbohydrate foods while avoiding fried and fatty ones. Rest the day before the big ride and continue your high-carbohydrate diet. This six-day program will leave your glycogen stores brimming.

50. If you're unfit, don't bother to carbo load. Your muscles won't store more than their usual amount of glycogen, and any extra carbohydrate calories will be converted to fat.

51. If your legs feel stiff and heavy after carbo loading, don't worry. This is normal because high levels of glycogen cause fluid retention in muscles. Once you start lowering glycogen levels by cycling, the discomfort will disappear.

52. Following a ride of more than 2½ hours, which will deplete your glycogen stores, eat a high-carbohydrate meal. This refueling will enable you to ride well again the next day.

53. When you're well into a long ride and need to stop at a convenience store for food, here are the best choices (remember that a cyclist's diet during a regular training season should be at least 55 percent carbohydrate and only 30 percent fat).

- Snack items: The best choice is a bag of pretzels (salt-free if possible). Unlike nuts and seeds, they aren't naturally high in fat. And unlike chips, they aren't fried. An ounce of pretzel sticks gives you about 110 calories, 81 percent from carbohydrate.
- Cookies: Fig bars are the wisest selection. Each one gives you about 50 calories, 83 percent from carbohydrate.
- Candy bars: Most have an unacceptable 50/50 ratio of fat and carbohydrate. The exceptions are Milky Way,

which is 66 percent carbohydrate and provides 260 calories, and 3 Musketeers, which has 250 calories but only
6 grams of fat.

- Pastry: Believe it or not, the best choice in this category
may be that old junk food standard, Twinkies. Two of
them provide 286 calories, of which 68 percent come
from carbohydrate and only 26 percent from fat.

- Ice cream and yogurt: Of the 167 calories in an ice-
cream sandwich, nearly two-thirds come from carbohydrate. Yogurt is even better, though. A cup of fruit-
flavored, low-fat yogurt (225 calories) is 75 percent carbohydrate and only 10 percent fat.

- Cold drinks: Sports drinks such as Gatorade are the best
choice. All their calories are carbohydrate, and most
brands replace potassium and other elements lost in
sweat. Also, they're designed to reach your bloodstream
quickly.

- Fruit: For endurance and nutrition, this is the best choice
of all. Fruit is nearly 100 percent carbohydrate and a
good provider of vitamins, minerals, and fiber. A banana
supplies 100 calories, an apple about 80, and an orange
about 60.

54. When taking a midride break at a fast-food restaurant,
choose one that offers pizza or Mexican. Four slices of a
12-inch cheese pizza (653 calories) are 59 percent carbohydrate and just 17 percent fat. A bean tostada (179
calories), an order of beans and cheese (232), or a bean
burrito (350) are each more than 50 percent carbohydrate
and less than 30 percent fat.

55. Don't bother taking vitamin supplements, scientists say, if
you're doing it for improved performance. Vitamins do not
provide a direct source of energy, but they can help people
with nutritional deficiencies stemming from poor diets.

56. Instead of taking expensive amino acid supplements, get
all the aminos you need by eating protein-rich foods such
as chicken, fish, and dairy products. Besides, the claims
that amino acids increase muscle mass and decrease body
fat are unproven.

57.   Beware of "vitamin B$_{15}$," which is no vitamin at all. Sometimes referred to as pangamic acid, it has no chemical identity. Thus, a company can market anything it wants under the name B$_{15}$ and claim, as is typical, that it increases the body's ability to use oxygen.

58.   Unlike with caffeine or other performance enhancers, you won't get an energy boost by drinking alcohol before or during a ride. When your liver is busy processing alcohol, it decreases its output of glucose, thus limiting this important muscle fuel and causing premature fatigue during exercise. Meanwhile, the alcohol that's waiting to be processed by the liver is unable to provide any energy for the muscles. Even if it were available, alcohol is a weak energy source because it doesn't contribute to the formation of muscle glycogen—the body's preferred fuel for cycling.

59.   Drinking beer is a poor way to carbo load. Twelve ounces provides a scant 50 calories of carbohydrate, so drinking five beers (enough to make you legally drunk in most states) provides enough carbohydrate to ride only about 10 miles. Wine is an even worse choice. A 4-ounce glass contains just 15 carbohydrate calories. The poorest carbo loader, however, is liquor, which has no carbohydrate at all.

60.   To avoid putting on excess pounds during the Christmas and New Year holidays, and putting yourself in worse shape to start a training program for the new cycling season, follow these tips.

- Avoid overloading on empty calories by making your first party drink a nonalcoholic beverage such as mineral water or diet soda. This will begin to fill you, thus curbing your thirst. You'll avoid empty alcohol calories, and your appetite won't intensify as it usually does when you drink too much.
- Use willpower to limit sweets and fatty treats until you've had a nutritious meal, then you won't feel like eating as much.
- Go easy on sauces, creams, dressings, butter, and gravies. These are all pervasive sources of fat calories. Instead, use products such as low-fat margarine and no-fat salad dressing.
- Schedule your big meal for early in the day. When you

go to bed soon after eating, there's no immediate need for the calories you consumed. Thus, they're more likely to be stored as body fat.

- Don't starve yourself in preparation for the feast. Have low-fat meals or snacks beforehand. You'll still enjoy dinner, but you'll be less likely to overindulge.
- Help yourself to nice-size portions, then just say no to seconds. You'll always feel fuller a few minutes after eating than immediately after the final forkful goes down.
- Get some exercise, even if it's just riding the indoor trainer. This will burn some calories and help you feel positive about yourself despite some certain—though let's hope limited—dietary indiscretions.

61. Having a healthful diet doesn't mean avoiding fatty foods altogether. Enjoy them occasionally. Consider them a reward for being a cyclist. Then return to low-fat foods, which, along with regular exercise, are the basis of a sound diet.

62. When adding more oat bran or other fiber to your diet, here are three caveats.

- Increase intake slowly to let your digestive system adjust.
- Drink more water.
- Go easy on high-fiber foods the night before and the day of an important ride so as not to upset your system.

63. If you're trying to decide between carrying fruit or fruit juice on a ride, you're better off having both. Juices have about twice the water content as whole fruits, which can be helpful because it decreases the chance of dehydration. However, juices contain negligible amounts of dietary fiber. Whole fruits have a lot of it, which is why they're more filling. In terms of carbohydrate calories, half a cup of any fruit juice provides approximately 60, about the same as a medium-size piece of fruit.

64. Keep your on-bike drinks cool by using an insulated water bottle or other device. Temperature not only plays a role in a drink's taste but also its effectiveness. A cool beverage is refreshing, and studies have shown that cold liquids lower core body temperature. Plus, it's quickly digested and gets to work faster than a warm solution.

 CREDITS

Photographs and Illustrations

Carl Doney/Rodale Stock Images: photo 1-1; Fred Zahradnik: photo 1-2; Stan Green: photo 6-1.

Sally Onopa: illustrations 1-1, 1-2, 4-1, 9-1; Catherine Reed: illustration 6-1.

Rodale Press, Inc., publishes BICYCLING, America's leading cycling magazine.
For information on how to order your subscription,
write to BICYCLING, Emmaus, PA 18098.